Charles Beadle

A trip to the United States in 1887

Charles Beadle

A trip to the United States in 1887

ISBN/EAN: 9783337143138

Printed in Europe, USA, Canada, Australia, Japan

Cover: Foto ©Andreas Hilbeck / pixelio.de

More available books at **www.hansebooks.com**

A TRIP

TO THE

UNITED STATES

IN 1887

[*Printed for Private Circulation.*]

DEAR MOTHER,

As you said you would like to see the diary I kept during my trip to America I have had it printed.

It is I fear very imperfect, but will nevertheless give you a good idea of what we saw, and my opinions of the different places we went to. It may even be a little contradictory, as the people and the States vary so much from each other that opinions formed in one State may be to some extent modified or altered when visiting another.

However, if it gives you the least pleasure to read, you know it will be a sufficient reward to me for the trouble I had in keeping it.

                Yours affectionately,
                    CHARLES BEADLE.

BELVEDERE, *September*, 1887.

A TRIP TO
THE UNITED STATES.

I HAVE been for some time thinking of paying the United States a visit, for two reasons, the first being that my son Charlie has now been there with his wife for two winters, and I am anxious to form my own opinion of his prospects; and the second that I have a great desire to see what our go-ahead friends on the other side of the Atlantic are like in their own country, and to pick up as much useful information as I can from them. I think, also, it will do my boy Frank, who is to go with me, good, and will open his mind considerably.

We started on the 18th March to Liverpool, and slept the night at the Compton

Hotel. At three o'clock on Saturday we went on board the steam tender which took us to the Cunard steamer *Etruria*, the fastest and nearly the largest ocean steamer afloat. We left the Mersey about 5 p.m., and called at Queenstown for mails the next day. Soon after starting we had our seats at table allotted to us, and afterwards sat down to a splendid dinner, which we much enjoyed.

I must now describe the ship, as it is the first time I have made a voyage on one anything like it. She is 505 feet long, 56 feet beam, and with 13,000 horse-power, sufficient to drive her from twenty to twenty-two miles an hour in any reasonable weather; her tonnage is over 7,800; she is licensed to carry 1,040 passengers, has 16 boats, and 1,340 life-belts, so I expect the latter is supposed to be the total number of people on board when she is full. The upper deck is clear on each side for a walk of 110 yards, so that you can get plenty of exercise. The next deck has in the fore-part a music-saloon, with a piano and organ in it. It is beautifully fitted, and capable of seating, say, 150 people. Then comes the staircase, a double flight of stairs, very roomy and pretty, leading down to the chief saloon, which is capable of seating 370 people. Further aft is another good staircase, and large, beautifully fitted smoking-room; and beyond this the engines.

The state-rooms, or passengers' private cabins, each having two berths, are very nicely fitted with everything necessary. There are also several bath-rooms, a barber's shop, and in fact everything you can possibly want.

The deck under this has again a smaller dining saloon and a good many state cabins. The second-class accommodation is quite aft and not bad, although it will not do after the first, and the steerage is only endurable in case of necessity.

The thing to do on coming on board is to go to the second steward and get him to give you your place at table, which you keep, if you are well enough, during the voyage; and then to the bath attendant and fix the time for your bath—at the tick of the clock he comes to you to say it is ready. And splendid bath-rooms they are, with every convenience. I don't know how many there are of them.

This all sounds grand, but the one thing needful to enjoy it is to be a good sailor. This we neither of us turned out to be. The second night was a very bad one, and the ship rolled to such an extent that nine out of every ten were ill, and the remainder fit for nothing. Poor Frank is still in bed, and has not yet had a mouthful of food he has been able to call his own for five minutes; and I, although not really ill, have been sick and altogether upset, and to mend the matter, on the second morning I lost my foothold on deck, and in one of the lurches slipped down to the side of the deck with such force that on striking a spar lashed there, I broke my nose and blackened my eyes, so that while I am writing this I am anything but a reputable-looking person. I was taken in to the doctor, who is a very nice little man. He set my nose for me and told me there had been several other accidents of a trivial character. I am now known among the passengers as "the man with the broken nose," another man is known as "the man with the broken head." However, I think this little matter has been the excuse for several of the passengers to address me and make my acquaintance. I shall try to describe some of them later on. Most of them seem quite ready to tell you their history, their present means, and their future prospects, and many all their family affairs, which in some cases are very amusing. One, for instance, a man of about fifty, is going to America to look up his father, who is on the Stock Exchange there. The old man makes him a good allowance, sufficient for him to keep his wife and family and an establishment in France, and even to go in for trotters and racers, but, although seventy-eight, is one of the largest operators in Wall Street. He allows his other sons more than my friend, and they keep very large establishments, and as he had just seen in the paper that his father had lost £100,000 in one speculation, was going over to see what it meant, and he wanted my advice as to how he had better play his cards. Another young man at our table is a native of Holland, not a bad sort of fellow, I should think. He made a start for himself early in life. Although he is now not above twenty-five, he has a business as grease merchant in Chicago, and has promised to take us over the various establishments there. He says he came into a good bit of money on his own account, a year or two ago, which he made over to the other members of his family, as he had established himself and could do without it. I dare say we shall see more of him.

Then there is a Mr. Stanley, who brought an introduction. He has been making railways in India and other parts of the world, and is now on the look out for a gold mine—something in Mexico. I expect I shall know more of him too. There is a young Canadian possessed of a large estate and ample means, but who broke up his health by nursing his first baby, as they were afraid to trust it to anyone else. He got up three or four times in the night to feed it for nearly six months, and has not been able to sleep since; and as he cannot stand the Canadian weather, he has to spend the winter in a hotter climate, which is sometimes in the south of Europe and sometimes in Brazil. Anyhow, he is always obliged to leave his wife and family for four months in the year when it is cold, and as his wife cannot stand the hottest months, she has to leave the estate for the sea-shore. They are very fond of one another, which makes it all the worse. However, he is looking forward to the time when the children are old enough to travel, so that they may all go to the south of France in the season, together. It certainly does seem an unfortunate case as it stands.

March 21*st.*—Until now we have had a bad

passage—430 miles first day, *i.e.* up to 12 o'clock yesterday, and 380 to noon to-day. It was so rough last night the engines had to be worked very slowly for many hours. As it was, the water came on board and all down into our state-rooms, which I should have thought, in such a ship as this, would have been impossible, as the sea is not very high. It must have blown hard, however, as one of the sails was split all to pieces. Frank is still in bed sucking ice. I hope he will soon be able to take some nourishment.

24*th*.—The voyage so far has not been what might be called a pleasant one; the people are agreeable enough, but the weather is what the boys would call beastly. The roll has by degrees turned into a pitch. We had one fairly fine day, but all the rest of the time has been wet, cold, and rough. This enormous ship sticks her nose into the waves as much as my launch would do, or more; in fact, we have not had a sea the launch would not have lived in, and yet our funnels are coated with salt to the top. I have come to the conclusion it is not the size of the boat that makes her a good sea-going one. I expect the fact is that driving a boat at over twenty miles an hour cannot be made comfortable going, except in smooth water. We are, they say, considerably behind in our daily runs, and shall not arrive in New York until Sunday at earliest. Frank is still very sick. I shall be glad to get him on shore; as yet I cannot get him out of the cabin. Certainly the weather does not encourage him to move; for as I am writing this in our little cabin sitting on a portmanteau, with Frank on the sofa, the stern of the boat comes out of the water every few minutes, and allows the screw to run round in such a way that you would fancy everything would break to pieces. The engines are, as I said before, very powerful, and it takes over 300 tons of coal a day to drive them. To-day, to add to our enjoyment of the voyage, there has been a fog, and the whistle has been blowing at intervals. Moreover, we have seen some ice, not much out of water, but the sailors say there is no telling how much there is just underneath, and so they are keeping a sharp look out.

Last evening, although rough, we had some good music in the music-room; if the weather is fine enough, we are to have an entertainment to-morrow. I think I shall begin some letters for home to-night after dinner.

26*th*.—Have just (3 P.M.) taken the pilot on board, 300 miles off New York. Good enterprise to be knocking about so far out at sea for a job in such weather. It is very difficult to know what to do to amuse oneself even on a short voyage. I don't know what I should do on a long one. I suppose I should go in for some regular occupation. Many passengers amuse themselves by drawing lots for numbers every night, each paying 5s., the one that gets the number nearest to the number of miles run by the boat from noon that day to noon the next, takes the pool. When the pilot boat came in sight the betting was as to whether his number would be an odd or an even one, and then as to whether he would put his right or his left foot on to our vessel first.

Last night was about as wild as it could be, blowing very hard right in our teeth, and lightning every minute; and as the vessel dashed into the waves at her enormous speed, the water flew in all directions. I stood on the deck under a shelter for some time and never saw anything grander. I should say this boat could not last very long, the strain on her must be too great; she shakes from stem to stern, and as you sit in her cabins, with everything creaking and twisting, you want good nerves to believe it to be all right. However, as I write, and the water is smoother, she is like a floating palace, and you cannot help being proud of the nation that can turn out such a vessel and run her against such odds as if it were a matter of course.

I am now about to pack up ready for landing, which we hope to do early in the morning.

27*th.*—We sighted land early this morning, but could not get over the bar until nine, and then we had to wait to go through all the formalities. First the mails were landed in a small steamer with walking beam-engines; then the health officer came on board; then the Custom House officers, and after this we steamed up to the ship's berth at New York. The captain put her alongside a jetty as easily as we put colliers alongside the wharf at Erith. We were quickly on shore, but an hour before we got our luggage examined and away. The system they have here is a very good one: officers come on board before you are able to land and take the declaration of each passenger as to the number of his packages and their contents; a mark is put on them with the initial letter of your name, and when it is landed you have not much difficulty in finding it. An officer is deputed to examine them, and if your declaration is correct, you are off without further delay.

We took the omnibus to the Windsor

Hotel, and were in time for a late lunch; after which we went out for a walk, and after dinner went to bed early, as we were tired.

The entrance to New York from the sea I like very much. The statue of Liberty stands on a little island facing the entrance, and then the two fine rivers which have New York between them branch off right and left; and they are fine rivers, and what is more, the tide rises and falls so little as compared with our coast, that the boats can be kept afloat alongside piers, and hence docks are unnecessary. Each company has its own landing stage, and really the water frontage has a most business-like appearance. The water is covered with steamers of all sizes.

29th.—We got up in good time; after breakfast went down town, saw the public buildings and general character of New York. The Brooklyn Bridge is certainly the finest thing to be seen. It is, I should say, more than a mile long, has two lines of rail, two cart roads and a wide foot-passage over it, and is the best designed thing of the kind I have ever seen. Frank is writing a description of it, so I shall not.

The peculiarities of New York, as far as I have yet seen them, are that the roads are bad, and the paved footpaths abominable. The telegraph poles quite spoil the appearance of the streets; they are not poles but large trees, and are stuck everywhere; and the overhead rails, although useful, must be the greatest possible nuisance to the people who occupy the houses they run past.

The houses and shops generally are not so fine as I had expected, but there are a few which I suppose are specimens of what will be seen in a few years—very fine indeed. In the overhead railways you pay 5 cents ($2\frac{1}{2}$d.) as you pass on to the platform, and get out where you like; there are stations about every quarter of a mile. The trains run without signals, and follow one another so quickly that they are never more than two minutes apart, and always seem to be full. They do not stay at a station more than half a minute at the outside. We have been in them several times to-day. For two or three hours in the morning and evening they run still more frequently.

This hotel is not so very large, but the arrangement is very peculiar. There is an immense hall open to all comers, and out of it rooms of all descriptions, also open to the public. In the hall are bookstalls, post-office, telegraph-office, railway booking-office, office for theatre tickets, and everything you want. On the next floor are the dining and drawing rooms, very warm and comfortable and beautifully carpeted. In fact, the corridors and all are in one; there are no doors, and you can sit about in at least a dozen rooms, all leading one from the other. They charge so much a day, and have meals going on all day, except for about two hours in the afternoon. I should think there are fifty well-cooked dishes for breakfast to choose from. They never ask you for your number, and, in fact, feed all comers. To-day I said I expected a friend to dinner, and asked what I was to do. I was told it was not necessary to do anything. If he was with anyone staying in the house, he would have his dinner as a matter of course. The dining-room has, I should think, four hundred dining in it at once, and the attendance is splendid.

We met two young Scotchmen to-day on their way to Dakota to their farms. They say they have between four and five thousand acres out there for growing wheat. They put their crops in next month, reap it in July, market it before winter sets in, leave two or three men with the horses, and return to Scotland to spend the winter. They can get there now in ten or twelve days from Scotland, and it works and pays very well.

30*th*.—We called on Mr. Matthews and went up to the top of Mill's building yesterday. I got a good view of the city. Afterwards we called on Captain Green, Vice-President of the Barber Asphalte Company. He gave us a great deal of information, took us to Delmonico's to lunch, and afterwards met us and took us over the asphalte works in New York, where the Trinidad pitch is refined and made suitable for the asphalte; nice works and well laid out. We returned to the hotel, and then went to see Barnum's place, where the amusements were carried on with the utmost vigour, not a moment being wasted, and there were three or four different exhibitions in some cases at same time.

30th.—We took the 9.50 train from Buffalo. This train is the best I ever travelled in; it does the journey of 440 miles in eleven hours or a little less, *i.e.* forty miles an hour, including stoppages, which are only four in the whole distance. The drawing-room car seats thirty-six in comfortable arm-chairs fixed on pivots. At Albany they take on a dining-car with dinner laid for fifty, and give you choice of several good dishes (hot), including soup and fish, and as many dishes as you like, and fruit and coffee after, for 1 dollar (4s.) per head. There are smoking and washing rooms; you can get wines of any sort on board, and can walk from one end of the train to the other while going at full speed. We were a few minutes (under ten) late at Buffalo, at which some of the passengers grumbled. I am told there is to be an extra carriage run on this train, with bath-room, barber's shop, and several other conveniences on it. Those going on to Chicago can sleep in the train, and get there at ten next morning.

We found my son and his wife at the station; had some supper together at the Genesee Hotel, and walked home to their house, which is over a mile away.

31*st.*—Had a good look round Buffalo. Lunched at the hotel; afterwards, Mr. Albright, Mr. Barber's partner, and Mr. Warren, the manager, came round in Mr. Albright's carriage to take me for a drive round. The roads in the town are as bad as they can be. Those in the outskirts have many of them been paved with asphalte (Barber's), and are certainly very nicely done. The horses stand better on this asphalte than any other, and if it is as durable, it must come more into use. He also took me to look at Lake Erie, which is narrow at the Buffalo end. We looked at the coal-loading arrangements and the docks. Saw a very good system of feeding boilers to burn small coal and avoid smoke, of which I shall get full particulars. We then went to my son's house to tea, had some music, and returned to hotel to bed. To-morrow, if fine, intend to go to Niagara Falls.

April 1*st*.—This morning we went to Niagara as we intended; it is only about twenty miles from Buffalo. On getting out of the station we were very much bothered by touts, who were anxious to drive us round. They were so persistent that it became quite a nuisance, and we declined to employ one. There is no difficulty in finding out everything to be seen, and there is no distance to walk. We went first on to the island above the falls (Goat Island), as there is a bridge from the States' bank on to it. From it you get a capital view of both falls. I was not at all disappointed in them, though I was told I should be. There was a large amount of water, in consequence of the melting of the snow. We could not get down into the Cave of the Winds, in consequence of the ice. The sight was very grand; the rapids on the top, before the water reaches the falls, are almost as impressive as the falls themselves, and from the little islands in them, connected by light bridges with Goat Island, they can be seen to perfection. The enormous power of the falling water is astonishing. It has been estimated at 4,500,000 horse-power. At the foot of the falls hills of dust ice had grown up to the height of a hundred feet or more; we were told it would take two months to melt them. After looking at the falls from the States' side, we walked over the suspension bridge and had a look from the Canadian side. As the wind was blowing the spray on to that shore, we should soon have been wet, but all the same we had a first-rate view of both falls at once, and it is a sight that once seen will always be remembered.

We returned to Buffalo about three, had

dinner early, and walked down to my son's house.

Called on Mr. Letchworth, and arranged to meet him to-morrow morning to go over his ironworks, which are, I am told, the best in the city.

2nd.—Spent the most interesting day I have yet had. Met Mr. Letchworth at ten, and he took me down to their works. They make all steel work connected with carriages and harness, and have works covering as much ground as Easton's; but the work is quite different, the castings they make in most cases not weighing more than a few ounces. He tells me the average value of these castings is not more than about 3d. per pound when finished. They are all made of malleable steel, which is cast very much as iron is cast, except that the furnaces used are more like ovens, and that the fuel is not mixed with the metal, but the metal is melted by heated gases passing over it. The ovens hold about six tons of metal at a time. The castings are at first as brittle as glass; they are then roughly cleaned, and put into iron saggers with charcoal and oxide of iron, and baked at considerable heat for about three days, by which time they are soft enough to bend about as easily as wrought iron. Each baking is tested to see that the temper is right. The little articles are then placed into revolving cylinders with small sharp stones, sand, and water, and are made to revolve very quickly for some time. When they come out they are sufficiently polished, and ready for use. They make very large quantities of everything connected with the trade, and export to Australia. They have a thousand acres of forest in Texas, whence they get the wood they want. They have also some very useful wood-working machinery. After lunching with Mr. Letchworth, junior, at his house, and being introduced to his wife and little girl, he took me to the prison. Till recently they hired the convict labour for a number of years, and used it on their works. I went over the prison, which is not, I suppose, very different to any other. They have cells about 6 feet by 5 feet, with strong iron bar gates, and some of them seem to be comfortably furnished, and have pictures and ornaments in them. The inmates do the washing and cooking. The chapel is divided down the middle by a large partition, from the pulpit to the end of the room, to separate the sexes. The Roman Catholics meet at 8, and any of the inmates can go to the service; the Protestants at 9.30, and any of the first batch can stay on to hear the other side of the question. The consequence is the chapel, which is a large one, is crowded, as I suppose it is a change for the prisoners, but I should fancy their religious notions get a bit confused if the preachers have the same amount of tolerance for one another they have in England.

The workshops are now no longer required for the use of the prisoners. The Knights of Labour have decided it is wrong for prison labour to compete with the free men, and the consequence is the prisoners are not to be employed in that work, and Messrs.

Letchworth have to move all their plant, which is extensive. They are now working with free men, and building new works in another place for that portion of their business.

After that a horse and buggie were put at my disposal. I drove down to the bank, and then to the house of the senior partner, who had asked me to call on him. I should think he was one of the leading men in Buffalo. His house, which is a very fine one, in the best part of the town, is beautifully furnished. I was shown into what I suppose was the drawing-room; the lower part round the walls to the height of about 4 feet was fitted with book-shelves, and filled with a splendid library of books. From there to the ceiling the walls were covered with well-chosen paintings and works of art, and the taste displayed in the whole arrangement was most finished.

I was at once made at home. Mrs. Letchworth, who is much younger than her husband, had her children sent for, so that I might see them, and two ladies staying in the house were also introduced to me. I should say they are a well-educated, superior family. They pressed me to stay to dinner or spend Sunday with them. However, I got back to the hotel, but not until I had promised to call again on my return, if I came into Buffalo.

3rd.—Sunday. Got up rather later than usual. Went to a church at which there was very little praying, but a very long sermon from a man who studied effect rather than matter, and would have done well for the stage. Afterwards we went for a walk. My son and his wife came to dinner with us, and we went later on to tea with them. We start early to-morrow for Pittsburg. Had a good look at one of the elevators being constructed, and could see the construction of it. They are built entirely of boards, piled together in such a way as to form very deep bins, which are filled from the top and drawn off from the bottom. The one we saw seemed to be built without fastenings of any kind, and must have taken several large cargoes of boards to build it. Timber of all kinds is about half the price it is in England. The lake steamers, which in some cases carry 3,000 tons, are all built of wood. They are frozen up about five months in the year; they will not get to work for some time yet. The docks and craft of all kinds are much behind those in England, and a good bit out of repair. The snow is going away very fast, and the roads look better and the town has a much nicer appearance than when we came into it. To-morrow we go through the oil district, and over the ground the natural gas comes from.

4*th.*—Started at 8.10 for Pittsburg. First part of the ride by rail was not very interesting, as the fields were bare, and there was little else to look at. Later on we came to a lot of woodland, where the trees had been allowed to blow down and rot, the old stumps remaining by thousands. There seems to be the greatest waste of timber and land about here, and everything is most untidy and desolate. As we neared Oil City we found traces of the oil wells, mostly, however, unused. Then came Oil City itself, a strange place — pumps put up everywhere, and large tanks to hold the oil. It seems that only a small pipe is put down to each well, and a little engine and a very rough pump put up. The oil is then conveyed in pipes to places where it is refined, and these places are owned by large companies, who buy the oil of the small men and control the market. There is considerable waste, and the river—which all along here, and in fact to Pittsburg, runs by the side of the line—is covered with it. The town of Oil City is rather an important place, and the centre of a considerable trade.

Just after we left it we found the first indications of the natural gas, which was burning in several places to waste on the ground, not the least curious being a large flame from the top of the water in the middle of the river. The journey on to Pittsburg was a beautiful and interesting one, the banks along the river being high and well wooded. The oil wells have a scaffolding of timber not at all unsightly over each, and in many places there are small coal drops over the railway. Coal is found all along this district at a level of from 200 to 300 feet above the river; the seam is some six or seven feet thick and the coal good. As we neared our journey's end the symptoms of the presence of natural gas became greater. Villages were lit by it, common lamp-posts being placed at the corners of the streets, with a large torchlike flame to each burning day and night. We arrived about 7.30 at Pittsburg, put up at the Monongahela Hotel, which is large, and, like all the others we have been in, a kind of public meeting-place. We had very nice rooms given to us, and after supper had a look into the town. We went to bed tired.

5*th*.—Called on Mr. Veeder at ten o'clock. He received us with the greatest kindness, introduced us to his partners, and insisted on giving up a day or two himself to showing us about. After an early lunch, we started to look over the copper-rolling works he is interested in, which are the largest in the States. Nothing but gas is used in furnaces, boilers, or any part of the works. They smelt the copper ore into cakes, and afterwards roll it out to any size or thickness they require. I suppose it is chiefly used in making kitchen things. They have one department devoted to producing copper pails or boilers, which are made out of one piece of copper without a single joint. There seems to be a large quantity of gas used. I should say the gas must be cheaper than coal. Veeder puts the price at 2d. per thousand feet. They pay about £100 a month for it, which is a considerable saving on what they paid for coal previously. We also went over some ironworks next door, again run entirely by the gas. They are able to get any heat they like with it, and control it beautifully; but the pressure is so great that when it is not being used for business purposes, they are obliged to relieve the pressure in the pipes by burning it to waste, and on Saturday and Sunday they say it is a curious sight to see these places burning gas in jets throwing fifty feet of flame. Veeder says, if the gas fails they have made up their minds to make it out of waste fuels in Siemens' or other gas producers, as they find it so much more suitable for their work than coal. The engines are all high-pressure and non-condensers, and the waste of fuel enormous, and lamentable.

Pittsburg is most beautifully situated, and is a very fine city of nearly 300,000 inhabitants. The electric light is used more than gas in its streets and buildings, and is perfectly managable. There is a notice up in our hotel bedrooms that if gas is used it must be paid for as an extra; the electric lights, which we can turn on or off at pleasure, are free. The city is situated something like New York, being at the confluence of the Monongahela and Alleghany rivers. Both are very fine rivers and run something like 1,800 miles before their waters reach the sea. There is plenty of high ground round the city. We went to the top of one place on an inclined lift, and had a look at the city from a height of 400 feet.

6th.—Mr. Veeder met us and took us over the Bessemer steel works belonging to Mr. Carnegie. These are the largest works of the kind in the States, and are given up to making steel rails. They turn out, I think they told us, 400 tons a day of finished rails. The works are about twelve miles out of Pittsburg, are very well designed, and beautifully kept. The whole of the operations are controlled by men at a distance from the hot work, who stand on a platform in a corner. Hydraulic power is used everywhere, and nothing is done by hand that can possibly be done by machinery; and, which seems most extraordinary, there is very little dirt or dust about, as no coal is burnt, the most intense heat being procured by the use of the natural gas. It certainly does seem that the people of Pittsburg have succeeded in opening up a business communication with the Old Gentleman, and that he is furnishing them with as much heat for nothing as they can possibly use, and even waste. The pressure at which the gas comes up is, they say, in many cases over 500 lbs. to the square inch, and by mixing air with it in proper proportion it will melt anything. The boilers manage themselves; the fronts are painted in fancy designs and kept clean. I suppose these works are not better than those in Wales and other places at home, with the exception of having this unusual advantage, and being very well designed and constructed.

In the afternoon I went for a walk with Mr. Veeder to the cemetery where his wife was buried, and round that part of the country, from which we could see all over Pittsburg and the three rivers. We spent the evening at Mr. Veeder's house, and he did all he possibly could to make us at home and comfortable.

7*th*.—Got up early, and at nine started

with Mr. Veeder first to look over the glass-works, where they were making and moulding glass by means of the natural gas. We then went over Dr. Hussey's shovel works. These were managed by a Mr. Wilson, a nephew of Mr. Veeder's, and a thoroughly business-like young man he must be. The contrivances they have for doing the work at small cost are really wonderful. The whole of the buildings and machinery are as little costly as it is possible to fancy, and yet they turn out hundreds of dozens of the very best made shovels a day, and take the trade not only of the States, but of Canada, Australia, and other places, and have just appointed agents for London—Welsh and Lea, 60. Gracechurch Street. I have promised to send them out samples of shovels mostly used in England, and Mr. Wilson has promised to look into, and if possible take up, my brother's patent horseshoe.

The contrivances of cheap hammers, with indiarubber springs for starting them, the emery wheels for cleaning and polishing, which they make themselves by placing canvas on wooden wheels and gluing emery on to it, and also by gluing emery powder on leather straps, are useful and clever. We also went over Dr. Hussey's ironworks, which are very large, and the steel works, where all the best grades of steel are made; then over some nail works, which were extensive and in full work.

By this time we wanted something to eat, and returned to the hotel. We then went by appointment to the tube works, managed by a Welshman, who seemed delighted to see us, and asked us to come up again if possible. This is an enormous place; they make welded pipes from the smallest sizes up to eighteen inches in diameter. They were making ten-inch when we were there. The welding is done by rolling them when at a white heat over a ball at the end of a rod. They make splendid pipes. The smaller sizes are tested to the extent of 2,000 lbs. to the square inch, and the larger sizes to a high pressure, but not so high. The ends have flanges screwed on to them, which make beautiful joints. These pipes are in the States entirely superseding the cast pipes. The present cost of the ten-inch pipes is 1½ dollars per foot run, equal to 6s. This seems high to me. The activity in this place is great, and the quantity of pipes turned out must be very large indeed.

We are to start to-morrow early for Philadelphia.

8th.—Started as arranged; the first part of our journey for some hours was up hill, and most part of it along a river running back into the Ohio. After this, we got on to the highest point, which I suppose is about the lowest pass on the Alleghany Mountains; we ran through a tunnel for some distance and reached the watershed on the other side. Here is the famous Horseshoe Bend, and a beautiful view we had of it and of the valley beneath. A little lower down we came in sight of the river, which was at first a mountain stream, widening afterwards until it becomes in some places half a mile wide, but not deep enough to float a boat. As you near Philadelphia, the land is well cultivated, and the farmhouses remind one of those in England—well-fenced fields, and comfortable-looking places. The stations about here are pretty and well kept, and would compare favourably with most of those round London. The railway itself is the easiest riding one I have ever travelled on, and the drawing-room carriages are splendid. This time a kind of bar was fitted up at the end of the carriage, decorated with pretty china, and when we wanted refreshments, a table was fixed up between the chairs, and what was ordered brought to us; and although the journey took eleven hours it was quite a pleasure trip. We arrived at Philadelphia about seven o'clock in the evening, put up at the Lafayette Hotel, and after dinner had a walk, and went to bed.

9th.—Went to call first on Mr. Barber's friend, Mr. Warren, who was out, then on Mr. Childs, of *Philadelphia Ledger* renown.

He was very civil, showed me his office and curiosities, said he was to be from home to-morrow (Sunday), but offered me his pew in church, and asked me to dine with him on Monday, and said I must at any rate bring my children to see his office, which contains so many curiosities, and he would give my daughter-in-law a cup in remembrance of the visit. I thanked him, but told him I should be unable to accept his hospitality, but that having heard of him so often in England, I could not, having an introduction to him, pass without making his acquaintance. He is an extraordinary little man, and has, I should say, many good qualities mixed with some eccentric ones. Afterwards I called on Detricht, my brother-in-law, John Greig's old friend. He at once gave up his time to me, sent for Mr. Reany, and took possession of me for the remainder of the day. First, they took me to see the most interesting business buildings, of which there are many—banks and insurance offices in particular; then to Independence

Hall. This is a very interesting place: it is where the Declaration of Independence was signed. The room is the same (furniture and all) as when the deed was done. I suppose nothing would induce the people of the States to alter it in any particular. There are good portraits of the chief characters of the time, original letters from Washington and others, and many other interesting relics, and among them a bell cast in England in 1753, before the separation was thought of, on which was the following inscription: "To proclaim liberty throughout the land to all the inhabitants thereof." In 1776 the bell obeyed its directions, and was used to proclaim the freedom of the States. I could have spent a long time in this place. We then went over some large wholesale stores, the chief feature of which was the management, and among other things a capital arrangement of pneumatic tubes for conveying cash and bills for every transaction into the central office, and the receipt back to the customer. We then went to the splendid marble City Hall, partly finished, and paid for each year as it is built, so that there is no debt on it. They have already spent £3,000,000 sterling, and it will take another £1,000,000 to finish it. The tower is to be 500 feet high. They gave me a very good dinner, and then had a carriage ready to drive round Fairmount park, which is really very pretty for so new a place, and contains 4,000 acres, including the water of the river, which passes through it. This is where the exhibition was held; some of the buildings still remain. The rules are some of them good; for instance, if a party, rich or poor, takes possession of a spot for a gipsy party, or any other amusement, it is theirs, and no one else is allowed to go near it until they have done with it. We also went over the waterworks. The water of the Schulkill River provides motive power for pumping and water for the town, and the machinery is excellent and well kept. They insisted on giving me supper, and I must say it was the warmest reception I have ever experienced. John seems to have been a great favourite with them. They call him John, and seem to forget his surname. I should think he has quieted down a good bit since he was here.

10th —Got up late, went to the Methodist Episcopal Church. (There are hundreds of churches of all sorts in this city.) The service was strange to me—one long prayer, some singing, a lot of notices of what was to be done. An illumination of gas over the pulpit, such as you would see over a west-end shop on a Queen's birthday; splendid decoration of flowers, and a long, good sermon, but too much action and manner again. After midday dinner, called on Mr. Warren, 2013, Spurce Street, on Mr. Barber's introduction. He treated me, as everyone else has done, as well as it was possible. Introduced me to his family, asked me to bring my children, and spend remainder of the day and go for a drive to-morrow, which I could not do. Then went for a walk with me, took me to see some fine houses he had built, and a church with a kind of a club built on to it for the use of the members; a splendid place, having among other things chairs so arranged that they can be linked together and arranged in any form desired. He then took me over the picture gallery, where there are some fine paintings; over the club, which is as well found as any in London, and quite a large place; and came back to the hotel to be introduced to my children, Charlie, Polly, and Frank, and ended up by giving us all a pressing invitation to spend a week with him on Lake George, where he has an island and a house, and where the fishing is, he says, very good.

11*th*.—Spent the morning in walking again over Philadelphia and making a few purchases. Started at 4.30 for Baltimore, which is not more than a hundred miles away; the journey is along the Chesapeake River, over several pieces of shallow water, and through a country rather rough, which, if in England, would be good sporting ground. In this neighbourhood the celebrated canvas-back duck is found.

Arrived at Baltimore about seven o'clock, and found a wire from my wife. It is very nice to have these messages; without them I should not know anything about home. They are all well, I am thankful to say. She wants to know whether I will stand as churchwarden at Belvedere. I have answered, will do what Belvedere friends think best. The meeting is, I suppose, to-morrow.

12*th*.—Had a good look round Baltimore, which is a fine city and a large port. The streets are very well paved; the public buildings are large and good. Electric light everywhere. The shops, particularly the clothiers', large and gay. The climate altogether milder, although not far south of Buffalo. The one we left fast bound in ice, and find the other as warm as summer, with trees coming into leaf. Many river steamboats start from here. The water accommodation is splendid; something like Portsmouth, only much larger and further in from the sea. Tons of oysters are brought here; you can get them in any quantity at every meal. The shells are ground for chicken food or burned into lime. There was a wood-cutting machine here for firewood, which would cut and split a cartload as fast as cart could be loaded. The hotel (Barnum's) was a very large and old-fashioned one, but not the most comfortable.

We had splendid ice here. Ice making is a large business in the southern States; I should say it would pay in England. We started at 7.45, but left Frank's bag behind. I hope he will get it in the morning.

13th.—At Washington we put up at the Arlington. I spent this morning in going to the British Legation to swear to some documents, and in writing to London with them, and several other letters, and afterwards had a walk round the streets near the hotel. After lunch we went to the Smithsonian Institution in the park, where there are some very interesting things, particularly the casts of sculpture from Mexico, which seem to be as ancient as the Egyptian, and very much like them; in fact, you cannot help suspecting that in very ancient times there must have been some communication between the two countries. The various dresses and arms of the Indian tribes might also be studied to advantage, and the animals found in different parts of the States, or rather on the American continent generally. The Department of Agriculture must be useful, as not only are the seeds and products exhibited, but samples of the earth from various parts of the world which grow crops of plants not yet introduced into the States.

We also inspected the marble column erected, partly by subscription and partly by the Government, in memory of Washington. It is a plain obelisk, 60 feet square at the base and 555 feet high, and as far as I can see will not last long, as it is built entirely of marble and the bottom stones are being crushed by the great weight. After dinner we had a walk round the lighted streets before bed-time.

14*th*.—Received some letters from home, *via* Buffalo, but dated 20th March, so they

THE PATENT OFFICE. 45

must have been kept a long time. One from mother; I will answer it. They all seem to have fancied we had a bad passage over. We went again to the Smithsonian Institution, and afterwards to the Patent Office, where there are thousands of models of all sorts of inventions. It is necessary to make a model of everything that is patented, which has to be deposited before the patent is granted, although many are most absurd things. Some good ideas may be got if you had time to study them, which we had not. Frank's horseshoe is not yet in its place. Women are employed in the States much more than at home, and seem most intelligent and painstaking; they have almost entire charge of all these institutions. You find them shorthand writing or type-writing in almost every private office, and they earn in some cases 15 dollars, or £3, a week.

We spent the afternoon in visiting the Capitol, which is really the Parliament house, and a very fine, sensible, useful building it is. Both the Upper and Lower Houses sit in large rectangular halls, where every word spoken can be heard easily; each member also has a desk or, I should say, a small writing-table before him. In one of the halls, formerly used by the representatives but now only as a lobby, there are some most extraordinary echoes—the most extraordinary I have ever heard.

Charlie and Polly left us this afternoon to return to Buffalo. We did not much like parting, but they decided they ought to go back, and we thought so too. We will look them up again at Buffalo, if possible, as we come home. They both look better for their little change.

In the evening we went to the theatre, which is a nice house. There was a very good play well put on the stage.

15*th*.—I decided on doing some calling to-day, and went to Mr. Barber's office, but Mr. Warner was ill; I then called on Major Powell, who was out. So Frank and I had another turn round, chiefly to see the parts of the city we had not before seen.

The night turned out wet and we had a thunder-storm.

16*th*.—This morning, when we had had our breakfast, Mrs. Langdon called on us. She is, I should think, nearly eighty, but has as much go in her as a girl. She brought Mr. Barber's carriage, and said she had arranged to take us out, and so we went with her. She took us for a long drive, pointed out everything of interest, took us to Mr. Barber's house, which stands on a high piece of ground overlooking the city, and will be a nice place when finished, and then drove us to the Soldiers' Home, some distance further out. This is a very pretty place indeed, has a nice park round it, and is very well kept.

She went back with us to the hotel to lunch, and unfortunately had a fall down some stone steps, which I fear must have hurt her, but she would not acknowledge it, and went at once (walked) to the Corcoran Gallery of pictures, which we had not seen. Here another friend of Mr. Barber's met us;

they did all they could to induce us to stay over Sunday with them, but I thought we had better get on. Mrs. Langdon is a splendid old lady. She had just returned from a trip to Florida where she had been by herself, and she told me that two years ago she went to San Francisco with another lady on an excursion for a month, and lived and slept on the train the whole time. She seems inclined to go to Europe with us to join Mr. and Mrs. Barber; she is to let us know. We started at 4.30 P.M. for Richmond, where we arrived at 9.30 next morning.

17th.—The railway runs good part of the way by the sea and over shallow arms of it, and is rather pretty; the stations are, many of them, only stopping-places, without buildings of any sort. The conductor takes money, I suppose, as there are no station-masters or anyone else at these little places. The trains run through the streets without the least protection, and children play within a yard or two of them as they pass. The only thing they do is to slack speed and ring a bell when they get to a place where there are many people.

Richmond, Virginia, is a nice town and well situated. It is the chief place of the tobacco trade, and very interesting, as being so much concerned in the slave war. There are some finish streets and good buildings, and the roads leading out of the town on the higher ground have some good modern brick residences on them, built as much like such houses would be a little way out of London as you can well imagine. The square in the middle of the town, where the monument to George Washington stands, is well kept, and has several tame squirrels running about in it. They will feed out of your hand and run over you; one rather surprised me by running up my umbrella. I suppose we could tame them in England. There was nothing whatever to keep them in, but little boxes in the trees for them to sleep in. We went to the Episcopal church, where they had the English service with variations, some of course necessary, but many only for the sake of making them. There was no congregational singing. Three professionals were allowed to come in with their voices wherever there was the slightest chance; they had good voices, but a curious selection of music. The sermon was a good one, on the progressive nature of sin. In this church spittoons and fans were placed in each pew. We started by the 9.30 P.M. train from Richmond. There were no other passengers for the Pullman sleeping-car, so we had the whole to ourselves, and made friends at once with the conductor and attendant. The conductor, a well-educated man, who considered himself in every way equal to his passengers, sat down at the same table to dinner, had a bed the same as ours made up for him, and took his seat in the car as if he were, as I suppose he was, lord and master. The attendant, a black, was very attentive. Our beds were made up at once, and very comfortable they were, with curtains almost like a four-post bed of old, and full size and width. We slept well, were called an hour before we were due at the station, where breakfast was ready, and after a wash and shave we got there and enjoyed our breakfast very much. The railway ran through pitch-pine forests and over rivers and thickly wooded swamps, and then there were small patches cleared, and houses, or rather huts, for the black people. The beautiful pine-trees are being badly used: they cut a great gash in them near the ground, chop into them a third of the way and drain all the pitch they can out of them, and at last kill them, and then, as if to do them all the harm they possibly can, set fire to them. I was quite sorry to see many beautiful trees burning slowly in the heart, smoke coming out of holes here and there up higher. This has been going on I suppose for a long time, as there are hundreds and thousands of blackened stumps remaining. I never saw such waste of timber, and as it is near the coast I am sure something better might be done.

We saw the first cotton-fields along this trip. The flowers, azaleas and rhododendrons, were numerous, the former in full bloom, but no sign of bloom on the latter; thousands of wild flowers and very large creepers, such as you see in pictures of tropical forests. The rivers, of which we crossed many, are very pretty indeed, but I should say very unhealthy to live near. We reached Charleston at 3.30, and at once had a look round the town, as we could not eat anything. The town is situated, like most of these towns are, on a tongue of land between two rivers only five miles from the sea, and the harbour is as good as New York, and not unlike it, except that it is much smaller and there is very little going on. The houses all show the effects of the earthquake; the porticoes of the public buildings are most of them still in ruins. This hotel, the "Charleston Hotel," is a large one, and cracked all over. They have stopped up the cracks in our bedroom, and there is almost as much crack as wall. The dining-room ceiling seems to have been all down except a small piece in the middle. They say the main shock only lasted four seconds; a minute at the same force would have levelled every place in the city. The people even now seem very nervous. A policeman told us he heard or felt a shock almost every night, but that orders had been given not to mention or publish it, so that the people might be quiet.

They seem to have got low-spirited about this town. It was, they say, knocked to pieces in the time of the war; a year or two ago a whirlwind broke up everything; last year the earthquake did hundreds of thousands of pounds' worth of damage, and most of the places will have to be patched up; and now they fear an inundation, as the town level is very low, and they seem to think it stands on a bad foundation. Our policeman said he hoped for more thunderstorms than they had had lately, as it was his opinion they would draw the electricity out of the earth and thus prevent earthquakes. There were little machines on the dinner tables to fan away the flies. The black population, I should say, vastly outnumber the whites about here. They are very obliging and seem to be happy and contented; some have nice manners, and all speak fair English. I am speaking of those in the towns. There is a considerable quantity of cotton shipped from here. There is also a trade in pitch-pine timber, but not so large as at Jacksonville. I bought some photos of the ruins of the town after the earthquake.

19*th*.—We started to-day by train for Jacksonville at 3.30. The carriage, a Pullman sleeper, was all ours again, with three attendants; we made friends with them and got plenty of attention. The road was through a pitch-pine forest again, but shrubs became more tropical. There is only a single line of rails, other lines crossing it on a level. If trains come in sight at the same time at one of these level crossings the one that whistles first has first turn; if they both whistle together the man in charge of the crossing does as he likes. All the management seems to be rough and ready. Our train stopped on a siding to let an express go by, but as there was a poor woman in the express who had overrun her station, they stopped the express to let her get out and join our train. Conductors and several passengers got out of both trains, and I should think the operation took several minutes.

At one station where we were timed to stop twenty minutes, they told us if we liked to have a walk they would not go without us, as they were in no particular hurry. This the result proved; we were two and a half hours late at Jacksonville. However, we got there 8.30 on the 20th, and put up at the Hotel St. James; and a very nice house it is. Jacksonville is a pleasure town on the St. John's river. There is a little boat running up it, starting at 2.30, and returning at the same time to-morrow. We are going by it, as they say the river is about as characteristic of tropical scenery as any in this country. We went up as arranged in a little steamer called the *Manatee*. The boat was very comfortable, and the captain a most intelligent young man. We called at many landing-places on both sides of the river, the prettiest being that at East Mandarin. This is the place where Mrs. Beecher-Stowe lives, and a very nice little cottage she has. The houses, of which there are several, might be at Hampton or anywhere on the banks of the Upper Thames. The piers are all private ones, belonging to orange-growers, and it was very strange to see the pier-masters, most of them college men from England, dressed in white, attending the boat, and sending off their goods and friends. They seemed to be a family party on this part of the river. They get up early, do a lot of the work themselves, dine late, and afterwards take it in turn to have an evening at home. There is always a musical evening or private theatricals or some amusement on, and strange to say a Belvedere man is one of the party; he was on one of the piers and came on board and to Jacksonville with us. He says it is the most natural kind of life it is possible to lead. They have a splendid climate, nice houses, splendid river, always at nearly the same level and full of fish and wild-fowl. The forest on the banks round the clearings is composed of pine, oak, magnolia, mixed with all sorts of tropical plants and creepers. The settlers are almost all educated men and women, and the society is freer and better than you can get near London. We went up to a place called Green Cove spring, and put up at the Clarendon Hotel. The spring comes up from a deep hole, warm and as clear as crystal, just the thing to bathe in. We had a walk after dark. There were numbers of fire-flies, and as they turned they flashed almost as brightly as the stars. There is a good chance for a young medical man in Mandarin, as they are at present without one. The captain of the boat paid 1 dollar 75 cents per cord for his wood, which he used as fuel for the engine; they call a cord 8 feet by 4 feet by 4 feet. He pays his black men 15 dollars a month, and feeds them on rice, and a very little meat.

There is a law in Florida against shooting from a passenger steamer, or we could have shot some ducks. There is a 25-dollar fine for opening an oyster after the 10th of April, and a 50-dollar fine for opening a drain after March 10th, as it is supposed to be dangerous to health to do so in the hot weather. There is a good trade for a boat between Jacksonville and Nassau. She should not draw more than thirteen feet loaded, should accommodate a hundred passengers, and must have all the latest improvements as to machinery, and burn either wood or coal. Captain C. E. Garner, of Jacksonville, steamer *Manatee*, could manage her. I have promised to find whether there is such a boat in the market in England and to write to him. We got back to Jacksonville at eleven on the 21st, and took ferry boat and train to St. Augustine's, a watering-place on the coast, and the first settlement the Spanish made in America; there are in consequence some interesting buildings in it, a fort, &c., but the streets are nothing but deep sand;—altogether I did not think much of it. The most interesting sight was a tribe of Indians (Apaches), who had lately been a great trouble and had been taken—men, women, and children—and put into the fortress. There were about four hundred of them, and a wild-looking lot they were. The Europeans of all nations and Americans were very curious about them, and the dress of the European ladies seemed to astonish the Indian women as much as the want of dress in the Indian women astonished the ladies. We got back to the hotel about six (the Hotel St. James), and after dinner packed up for a start early to-morrow.

I found out an average orange-grove could be purchased at a pretty reasonable price now, ready to bear fruit; that it should be on the east side of the St. John's river, unless further south than this, when either side would do. The russet oranges are much the best. They grow strawberries, which are now ripe, but not good sorts. The land is nothing but fine white sand, and wants manuring for oranges or any other crop, but the climate is so splendid, anything with half a chance to grow will grow. It is a wonder to me how such splendid trees and shrubs can flourish as they do on such a soil. The streets of this town are a foot deep in sand, and except for boards laid along the paths, it would be almost impossible to walk.

22nd.—We started after a good breakfast at seven for New Orleans; all day the scenery was such as I have before described—woodland, chiefly fir, the wood being destroyed. As night came on, the line, which runs through Georgia for some distance, ran back again into Florida by the side of the Gulf of Mexico, and during the night through part of Alabama, which state we are told is to eclipse all others in the production of iron and coal, and has even more advantages than Pittsburg; but this I doubt. At any rate they have any quantity of iron and coal, both on the surface, or rather in the hill-sides. The line then runs into Louisiana. We arrived at New Orleans at seven on the morning of the 23rd. After a bath we had breakfast and walked to the side of the river, which is only three-quarters of a mile wide, but in some places 300 feet deep. The steamboats on it are the three-, four-, or five-tier river steamers so often described, but which will not much longer be seen, as the railways are running them off. There were, a captain of one of them informed me, ten times as many a few years ago. Now the largest remaining are laid up and have not moved a wheel for the last two years. We have decided to have a day or two on the river, so that we may know something about these wonderful boats before they become extinct.

23rd.—We delivered Mr. Barber's introduction to Mr. Tupper, of 81, St. Charles Street. He kindly introduced us to members of the Cotton Exchange—a fine building—and to the leading broker, Mr. J. Aldige, who has offices at the Exchange, who in turn introduced us to Mr. Maginnis, of the Maginnis Oil and Soap Works. This gentleman devoted much time to us, took us all over the works, and explained everything.

The cotton when it is grown has a seed round which the fibre hangs; this is partly cleared by the growers, *i.e.* they get off as much cotton as they can, leaving some still hanging to the seed. This comes down to their own and other mills, and goes through another process, by which 15 per cent. of the weight is saved in the shape of a good fibre, worth say 5 cents a pound, and is chiefly sold to Germany. The remainder is crushed, and from it they make the oilcake and many other products, including soap. The shells of the seed, still having fibre hanging on, is not used, but sold for cattle-food or burned in the furnace, and is only worth about 25s. per ton here. Two hundredweight of this can be packed in a large sack, so that it is not very bad for shipment. I arranged with him to pack ten tons and consign them to me in England. If it can be used I can get a hundred thousand tons per annum, and both Mr. Aldige and Mr. Maginnis will work with me. Promised to send them a copy of the Colonial Fibre Report.

NEW ORLEANS.

Ice-making is a great trade here. We went over a factory producing one hundred tons of splendid ice a day. They sell it at 5 dollars, or £1, per ton. This would pay in England, I am sure.

After dinner Mr. Tupper and a friend of his, a railway director, drove us round the town and district. There are some nice residences. It is, however, on very low ground—several feet below the level of the river, which, if it burst its banks, would sweep it away in no time. The town is older than any other we have seen except St. Augustine's, being one of the early Spanish settlements. There seems to be a very large trade going on.

On Sunday we went to the Episcopal church where they had an almost perfect English service; good sermon, only one hymn for the congregation but some professional singing again. We spent all the remainder of the day in writing letters. We were told by all, we could not get a boat to take us up the river until Tuesday night. We particularly wanted to go earlier, and by day, so we decided to board all the boats to see whether it was possible. We were rewarded for our trouble. We found a stern-wheeler whose business it was to go about seventy miles up and call at each plantation on the banks of the river, leaving or taking anything, from a letter to a steam-engine, where required. This was just what we wanted, and we at once engaged a cabin, and started at noon. The boat was like a large spoon, drawing about three feet of water, with an overhanging bow, so that she could run ashore. The boiler was on deck, as were also the engines. The cargo, which consisted of groceries, farm produce and implements, steam-engines, and many other things, was also stowed on deck. Over this, at a height of eight or nine feet, was another deck, supported on pillars; and on this were the sleeping and dining cabins and office. At one end of the dining-cabin was a piano; and there were couches and easy-chairs, and on the walls pictures and texts. Above this again was another deck, on which the captain and chief mate had their quarters. And then there was a kind of tower for the pilot-house, from which the captain directed his ship. The river is nowhere more than three-quarters of a mile wide, and the banks not more than six feet above the water; and as the boat had long landing-stages hanging from her bow, say fifty feet long, which she could raise and lower by machinery, she could land goods at any spot. She made thirty or forty calls before dark. Some of them did not take more than a minute. The cargo to go ashore on any given spot was got ready, and the blacks, of whom there were about twenty on board, ran on shore with it like so many ants, and then scrambled on to the stage as well as they could while it was being hoisted, to get on board again. They seemed to enjoy it as much as we did. But the best of it was, after dark the landings still went on, and we were surprised by seeing a great illumination all at once. This was a very strong electric light on board, driven by a separate engine, which could be directed in any direction on to the shore, and made everything as light as day. As the boat neared a landing this light came out, and as soon as it left the shore, disappeared again. It was a most curious sight to see the blacks running about in the light. It would illuminate for a quarter of a mile inland. When stuff had to come on board another light was set going on the deck. We were very anxious to see the cotton and sugar plantations as they were before the slave war, and this was the best possible chance, the plantations along this district being conducted as they were formerly, allowing for altered circumstances as to labour. The establishments are large : a good house in a grove of trees for the planter, quite a costly manufactory for the sugar-cane crushing, well-built and with considerable engine-power; a village for the blacks, now free people. The whole thing remains as of old —gangs working in the plantations with the

SUGAR PLANTATIONS. 67

overseer over them, driving them as well as he dare, but no whip. They can and do leave if they are not fairly well treated, and do not do so much work as they used to do, but still I should fancy do pretty well. We had a good look at many of the plantations, and a very fine chance of seeing and talking to the black people. Most of them speak French as well as English, and that is the case with all about here. Of course we got all the people in the boat interested in us. They laid a separate table at meals, and the captain or purser came to entertain us. We slept in a nice little cabin, and in the morning they arranged to land us at the nearest point to a railway-station, and after consultation decided on running the boat back some little distance, as they said in that case they could land us at a point called Convent, where we could get our luggage taken to the station. This they did. We had two or three hours to wait for the train, and walked round some of the plantations.

The cotton and sugar seem to grow best

on soil formerly left by the river, which extends say two miles on either side of it. It is below the level of the ordinary height of the water, which is used for irrigation. If the water rises too high it breaks the banks and ruins all the crops; if it falls too low, the land cannot be irrigated and the crop dies. That is what is feared now, as there has been no rain for a month. Our passage on the boat, including meals, cost us two dollars each. This is the first cheap thing we have met with.

26*th*.—We reached Convent station, as arranged, and travelled all the rest of the day to Vicksburg. Perhaps before leaving the sugar and cotton plantations I should give my idea of the negroes. They are very numerous here, much more so than the whites. They seem happy enough in their way. The women are fond of dress when off their work, and dress in the loudest manner possible; the dress-improvers and hats with feathers in them would be the envy of many of our Irish servant-girls at home.

Sometimes they even dress with some taste, and you are rather surprised on walking past to find a very ugly black face under the fashionable hat. In the fields, however, and among the older women, the dress as drawn in so many of the slave pictures is still the correct one. The men joke and laugh just as our mock nigger minstrels do, only "more so," and sometimes a gang makes so much noise that they attract the attention of every one near them. They are as a rule obliging and glad to have notice taken of them, and seem as sensible, and many of them as well educated, as their white fellow-creatures. In fact, I should think they would in time be entitled to rank with them, and be able to use the power they possess by the vote properly, although many seem to think voting power was given them too soon. I had no idea there were so many of them. They have entire charge of the waiting at several of the large hotels: one dressed completely up to the mark, with his gold watch and chain, &c., acting as manager of the dining-room and showing you into your seats. I found, however, a quarter-dollar was necessary to get attention; but this understood, they would pile plates of food round you until the sight almost made you turn sick. This reminds me that they ask for your order, and expect a list of dishes, which they will bring all together, so that you cannot possibly get a dinner without part being cold. If you order one dish at a time you have to wait between each while they are being cooked, which would take you hours, so we were obliged to fall into their ways. Vicksburg is a small town about 250 miles up the Mississippi from New Orleans, and a nasty little place it is. The hotel, the Pacific, is worse than the town; everything was filthy, and we were glad to get out of it. It was here one of the greatest battles of the slave war was fought, but it has nothing else to make it interesting. Memphis, a town five hundred miles farther up the river, is a much nicer place. We did not, however, stop there, but came on to St. Louis. The train is put on to a steamer at Memphis and taken over the river; the operation does not take long, certainly not half an hour, and is done very nicely. From there the road runs through a dreadful country, I should say as unhealthy a swamp as any in the world, full of snakes, small turtles, and animals of various sorts; snakes sunning themselves on logs of rotten timber. I never saw such an uninviting place. Alligator Creek and Bear Creek describe the stations. It is too early in the season to see the alligators, but they say there are thousands. We saw the skeleton of a monster, as he had died under a large stump. Thousands of trees, some very large, lie about rotting. Now and then a piece of ground is a little higher than the rest, and you find a hut or two and a clearing; but although fire is used to destroy the timber in every possible way, it seems almost impossible to get rid of it. Here sticks of oak which would be worth many pounds each at home, are rotting by the thousand or burning piecemeal. We were rather relieved when we found it time to go to bed. The carriage was very full, every berth taken, and too hot. There are some wonderful earth-mounds in this valley, built by some extinct race in far bygone times, worthy of study.

28th.—We arrived at St. Louis at 8 A.M., put up at the Lindell Hotel, got a nice room with a bath in it, had breakfast, and went out. First we took a tramcar and rode as far as it went into a pretty district, where there were some good residences and tastefully laid-out gardens, green and well-kept lawns. We then got into a tram moved by a cable seven miles long. It has a large enginehouse about midway to provide the motive power, and runs two cars together every few minutes, so that the power used must be very great, particularly as it winds round several corners and up and down hills. The outlay altogether must have been very considerable. It seems to work well, but I could not find out whether it was a paying concern.

In the morning had another turn round

ST. LOUIS.

city and along the water-side, and arranged for a start up the river on the following day. Saw Messrs. Warren & Co., Mr. Barber's friends, corner Fifth and Olive Streets, who were kind enough to give us some useful information. The river here seems to be as large a stream as it is at New Orleans, although it has between here and there lost several big tributaries; but I suppose it is not so deep. There is a very large business doing here, every one seems alive. The drygoods stores are numerous, and Cook's of St. Paul's Churchyard would not outdo some of them. The streets are well paved; electric light in common use; more telegraph, telephone, and electric power wires than in any other city we have yet seen. This is now a large place, and will soon get larger, as it is splendidly situated between the eastern and western States.

30*th*.—We left on board the *Gem City* (a steamer larger than the one we were on on the Lower Mississippi, but still not one of the best) to go up the river a little way. This boat was built like the last one I described, but had a much finer cabin on the upper deck, and had sixty state-rooms round the dining cabin, with two berths in each. The engines were for paddle-wheels, and the machinery was so much mixed up with the cargo that you could not tell which was which when the engine was not in motion. The beams, or rather connecting-rods, were of wood, thirty feet long, and with a five-foot stroke or more; she went very well, but at each stroke of the engine the whole boat bent, and, looking along her long cabin, it appeared like a slight swell of a sea, the deck heaved so much. The river above St. Louis is much prettier than it is lower down, one bank always high and the other a level left by the river, and now covered with trees. The little towns are pretty and clean; we passed several before dark.

May 1st.—In the morning we found ourselves a hundred miles or more up the river. We first intended to land at a place called Quincy, but decided on going higher up and got out about six at a place called Keokuk, a nice little town of some 14,000 inhabitants. We put up at an hotel on the water-side which turned out to be a very second-rate place, but they were very attentive, and gave us bed and breakfast for 75 cents each, which was the cheapest lodging we have yet had, and as we are out to see all sides of the question, were rather pleased with it than otherwise. The inhabitants of this town seemed to be nice sort of people; there were no end of places of worship, very well supported I think. As we landed, a very severe thunderstorm came up. I never saw more beautiful lightning. We went into a little Episcopal church; there were only about twenty in the congregation, and the old gentleman who preached was about as queer a person as I have ever seen, and preached a most extraordinary sermon on common things. He tried to be funny, but it was altogether a failure.

We had to get up at five next morning to start for Kansas City, and as our journey was over three lines of railway, had a fourteen-hours' ride. The country was altogether different from any we had seen—all good agricultural land, the first part in small farms well kept and nicely fenced, houses neat and tidy. As we got on, the fields were larger, and we could see we had struck the corn-producing districts; there were also many large fields with herds of cattle in them and some sheep. The towns and villages had a different appearance, and the people too, but all seem happy and satisfied, although they must work hard. A newsboy amused me this morning: on asking him whether he had a certain paper, he said, "Yes;" but after hunting through his packet he said he "guessed he had deviated," being his way of acknowledging he had not told the truth. The horses are all small, but nicely bred. The land is a dark rich soil; I should think it would produce several crops without much manure. The town of Kansas City has plenty of life in it; we shall see more of it to-morrow. I am glad to say I have letters from home up to 14th of last month, and I have telegraphed and hope to get a reply to-morrow. If all at home are well, we intend going on to the Pacific.

2nd.—Spent the day in Kansas City, a most interesting town; it is the typical city of the West, and a specimen of what has been done here. The place is only fifteen years old and has now 150,000 inhabitants. Steam tramways constructed at great cost and driven by means of a wire rope and large powerful engines in centre of the work, run round corners, and up and down steep hills, and are splendidly constructed. The ropes, seven or eight miles long, last only eight months. The fare is 5 cents, or 2½d., for any distance. They pay well. Trains run to all parts, and the river Missouri is navigable from the sea. There are fine buildings and splendid residences. The people are from all classes—cowboys, Mexican farmers, blacks, speculators, miners, and fashionable ladies splendidly dressed. I never saw a place so like making money, and one in which people seemed to be doing so well. A gentleman informed me it would not be much beyond the mark to say the people were on the average doubling their capital every year.

In the afternoon we went to see a base-ball match, and I am glad we did, for I wanted to see the game. The match was between Topeka and Kansas City teams, and I should say the play was good. It is a compound of rounders and cricket. A ground is marked out on any hard, flat place, turf not being necessary.

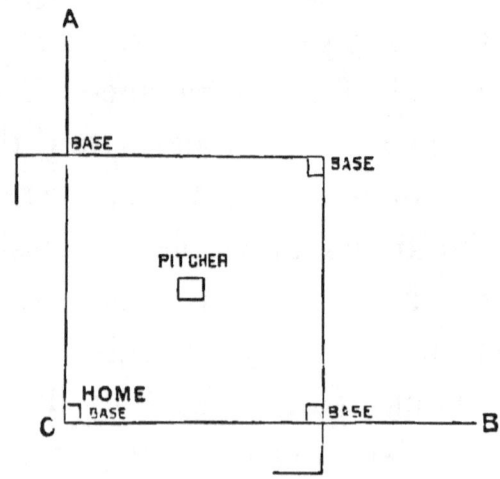

Base Ball Court.

BASE BALL.

They use an ash staff about the length of a cricket-bat, but round, and larger at the striking end than the handle. There are eight players on each side. The man that throws the ball is called the pitcher, and stands in the centre, throwing the ball as hard as he possibly can at striking height over point C, where the striker stands. If he hits the ball it must be sent between A and B, the fielders being placed out as at cricket. The first man runs as many sides of the square as he can on his hit. If the ball is thrown up to a fielder stationed at the corner before the striker gets there the striker is out, and the next man goes in; and the number of bases made—*i.e.* the number of men who get back to the hitting base—count one each on score. Each side has eight innings, and the total of the score on either side decides the game. Some of the catches were excellent, and the fielding was very fine, and I should say it is altogether a very good game.

4*th*.—We packed up this morning, and started at 11.15 for Salt Lake City. The distance is 1,280 miles, and we ought to get there on Friday afternoon. The first part of the way was not very interesting; but later in the day we got well into the open country and on to the prairies, and as night came on the prairie fires lit up everything round. It seems at this time of year they burn the old grass left over from last season to make it easier for the young grass to grow. The effect was splendid, but we were at last too sleepy to watch it and went to bed.

5*th*.—The morning found us 480 miles on our journey, and we arrived at a place called Pueblo to breakfast. There was nothing interesting here; it was, in fact, only a railway junction town, and we had to change cars, but we started at one o'clock for one of the most beautiful rides I have ever had. The railway was a narrow gauge (3 feet), but they had a very powerful engine and tender, fifty feet long together, and a Pullman car built to suit it. It is almost impossible to conceive how well the whole thing was done. The car was of course narrower than the ordinary ones, but still quite comfortable. The railway, a single line, was laid up the slope of the mountain in such a way that I suppose the grade did not at first exceed 1 in 50, and we went up at a fine pace, I should think thirty-five miles an hour. We were, however, soon stopped by a cow, but not before we had knocked her into the river. We were now so used to this that no particular notice was taken. After about two hours we came upon the mountains themselves, and dashed into them by the side of a mountain stream, or rather river, which had cut its way through the rocks. The cañon (as they call the clefts in the rocks made by the water) was so narrow that the place for the line had to be scooped out of the face of the perpendicular rock, and in one place a kind of bridge was hung on, so that we went right under the projecting rock and over the torrent. Up to the time the railway was made no man had ever passed up it, and men had to be let down from the top by ropes to construct the line. We had two or three miles of this kind of thing, after which the way opened out a little more, giving the engineers a better chance to make it. Farther in still, and higher up, there were little pieces of pasture and some huts and tents. Then we got to a kind of railway depôt, where our train was divided, two engines being put on to the first part, and our engine taking up the two Pullman cars, say a quarter of a mile behind them. The road was now very steep indeed, and wound among such sharp curves that you could constantly see the engine almost looking as if it were coming back to run into us, and as we kept sighting the first part of the train a little above us there were mutual greetings from the passengers. At last we met with cold and snow, and the line was protected by snow sheds; and then we reached the highest point in the pass— 10,850 feet. The air was so rarefied it made us all quite deaf. The train was here made into one again, and our two extra engines sent back, and we slid down the other side at about thirty miles an hour as easily as possible. It was getting late, but we had a beautiful moon. We stopped at a place on the mountain-side, where we had a good supper, and a little later, about ten, all turned into bed. My berth was on the river-side of the train (they always seem to follow the course of the rivers in making railways), and as the full moon was shining in at my window, and I could see almost as well as if it were day, I drew up the blind, perched myself up in the corner so that I could look out, and spent about an hour and a half in watching the river; and glad I was I did, as the exit from the mountains by the west side was much like that by which we had entered them, and by moonlight under such circumstances it was like a beautiful dream: splendid rocks, sometimes quite darkening the river, and then, again, the moon shining through on to the torrent or some waterfall, and we gliding down without steam and almost noiselessly. Altogether, I shall be a long time before I forget the delightful sensations it gave me. As soon as the best of it was past I fell off to sleep, and in the morning woke up to find we were in the most uninviting country I should think in the world—a plain without a bit of grass or herbage except a kind of wild sage, and here and there a prairie dog sitting up looking at the trains. I had no idea there could be such a dreadful place. It would frighten a strong man to find himself there alone, as it extends two hundred miles each way, I should think, the only break being at Green River, where a dirty river runs through it, and there are a few shrubs a foot or two high. As this is the only point at which the engine can get water or the passengers could be fed, the company have made a real station, and built a nice little hotel, which they have lit by electric light. They have made a garden and fountains, and they have managed to get a rim of grass about a yard wide, just where the fountain keeps it moist. But the people in the hotel gave us the best breakfast it was possible to desire, and seemed as pleased to see us as we were to see them.

We had had several hours through this kind of country, when we came on some more rough, uninviting mountains, up which we had to wind our way to the height of about 6,000 or 7,000 feet, and again met with snow. Then we opened on to the Salt Lake Valley, and the Salt Lake City at last came into view. These people, the Mormons, must have had good pluck to settle down in such a place. There are no natural advantages about it, except that the mountain-streams can be used for irrigation. They avail themselves of this one advantage to the greatest extent. Every street has a stream of water running on each side of it, and every garden has a spray of water playing on the grass. By this means vegetation is kept up, and I suppose the people manage to exist in tolerable comfort. Anyhow, the dinner here at the hotel was one of the best we have had in the States, and very well cooked and served. The game dish was black bear, which I tasted and enjoyed. The train leaves at 2 to-morrow. We shall have time to look round us before we start, and perhaps to bathe in the lake.

7th.—It was too cold for a bathe in the lake and some distance to get to it; we therefore took a carriage, with Mr. Todd and his wife, and drove round the place. The Mormons who are well-to-do have in some cases many wives, and have houses built one beside the other and a wife in each; but they say, not above one in fifty has more than one wife. In some cases they have many wives, and it does not seem to work so badly as might be expected, the first wife having to give her consent to any future marriage. The central government have now made these marriages illegal, and are punishing the offenders—several are now in prison. They have constructed a fort on high ground overlooking the town, and have some big guns and a thousand soldiers in it, so that I expect the Mormons will have to give in. However, it is quite on the cards there will be trouble over it, as there are five Mormons to every Gentile here. The Tabernacle, a very large building with an arched roof, will seat 10,000 people. You can hear a pin drop from the reading-desk when standing at any part of the building. This is a fact, as we tried it. The Temple is a very ugly stone building not half completed, but already thirty-two years in building. I should say it never will be finished. I fancy the whole thing is a swindle by the leaders on the people, who are uneducated. Emigrants are constantly coming in; five hundred arrived from Sweden and other countries last week. The Salt Lake is a large piece of water, very salt, about one-fifth being solid salt. It is a miserable place, and smells badly in shallow places in the sun. The lake is 100 miles long, and has an island in it 10 miles long. We started in the afternoon on a journey from Salt Lake to San Francisco, about 800 miles. It is not a nice ride, many hundred miles of it being over sand without vegetation; and as this lasted all Saturday night and Sunday, we got rather tired before we finished the day. We were in a most splendid Pullman car, a new one, but with a disagreeable attendant, and we did not enjoy our Sunday, although there were nice sort of people in the train. The feeding was at the stations, where good meals were provided at 75 cents each, and twenty minutes given to eat them. I would not be the keeper of one of these places on any condition. Some Indians found their way to each; they spoke English very well. The women are very ugly. They bring their packed-up babies (papooses) to be looked at at 10 cents a peep; one, on being offered 5 cents ($2\frac{1}{2}$d.) refused, and returned the money. One of the men, on being asked why the women painted their faces so much, said he did not think they were worse in that way than our girls out East. The Indians are allowed to ride free. When the line was constructed it was thought this privilege would induce them to protect it, and it is found to have that effect. We went to bed early, and got up at 4, hoping to get a view of the scenery on the ascent of the Sierra Nevada, but we lost some of it.

We, however, did see the top and the splendid country down into the valley of Sacramento. It is very fertile, loaded with fruit-trees and flowers. The town of Sacramento itself is fine but on low ground; the river is several hundred yards wide but dirty. The land from there to Oakland is flat but fertile. The train crosses the Sacramento river on a very large ferry-boat—I am told and believe the largest in the world; she brought over three engines and two trains of cars, and yet there was room. At Oakland we had to get into another splendid ferry-boat to take us over the bay, but this does not take the train over. This boat has a cabin on the upper deck more like a very large waiting-room at a railway station, large enough to seat several hundred people, and well-furnished with comfortable seats. She has a large crank engine with at least twelve-foot stroke. These boats run their noses into a space, enclosed by two rows of piles driven close together, made to exactly fit the boat. The piles are left so that they have a spring in them, and as the boat touches them in any place they spring her off until she is exactly in her berth, so exactly that the rails meet and the engines and carriages run on board without trouble.

9*th*.—On reaching San Francisco we went to the banker's to get some money, and to the agents to make arrangements for visiting the Yosemite Valley, which we find we can do, as it is just open. We took a steam rope-tram to the end of a long street running on to high ground, and then walked on to a hill overlooking the town, harbour, and ocean, so that we might see where we were and find our way about.

It is a fine city, and may be called the wooden city. I should have thought it almost impossible to build such splendid, well-designed, enormous buildings of wood. No wonder these places burn; the wonder to me is they do not all go when one starts. To-night the boys are crying full particulars of the fire, so I suppose there has been a large one somewhere.

We have put up at the Baldwin Hotel, a very fine place, but nothing like so large as the Palace Hotel, which makes up a thousand beds. Both these places are of wood, and wonderful places they are. Some travelling companions, Mr. and Mrs. Todd, came to dine with us here, and we went to the Palace Hotel, where they were staying, to hear the band in the covered courtyard there. Mr. Todd is a young engineer, but has broken up his business in the East in order to settle in a western town, as the only chance of saving his wife, who is consumptive. They are Americans of very good type, but under the circumstances a little low-spirited. A clergyman stopped us in the street. We came across the Atlantic with him, and now have run against him again, after having each travelled some four or five thousand miles since we parted.

10*th*.—Went with Mr. and Mrs. Todd to

the park, and on to the coast at a place called the Seal Rocks, where a fine view is to be had of the Pacific Ocean and coast. The harbour is a splendid one, large enough to take all the fleets in the world, and the entrance through the Golden Gate very fine indeed. There is an island in front to protect the harbour, something like Spike Island at Cork, and the harbour is not very much unlike it in many respects. The seals playing about the rocks are very numerous and large; they seemed to me more like sea-lions than seals. An old king-seal, well known, sat on one rock. He was much larger than the rest, and we were told was absolute lord and master of the lot. There is no law against shooting these seals, but good feeling and public opinion protect them. We had lunch at a place overlooking the rocks, and returned to the city to dine. After dinner I hired a guide to take us over the Chinese quarter of this city. There are, I am told, about fifty thousand Chinese here; one part of it is given up entirely to them, and they live I suppose much in the same way as they do in the low parts of the cities in China. The shops in the respectable streets are not at all bad, and seem to be kept by respectable members of society; but as we wanted to see everything, and we had as a guide a very intelligent man, who got his living in the daytime by interpreting for the Chinese who cannot speak English, and seemed to be well known, we got him to take us into some of the worst districts. First we went into a sort of temple where there were five of their gods. These were supposed to be the ancestors of the race this particular temple belonged to, and the records dated back some three thousand years, but from what I could see and find out I fancy it was more a sort of divining-room than a place of worship. There were vases filled with slips of hard wood, each having certain words on it. In cases of illness, it is the custom for them to draw out one of these pieces of wood; the word on it has then to be turned out on some scroll, and opposite the name of the medicine to be taken is given, and the patient takes whatever it may be. Then again there are pieces of wood, shaped something like a boat. These are thrown up, and if they fall in a certain way the question to be decided is favourable, if in another unfavourable. A tray of sand is kept, over which a kind of stick pointed at one end is suspended, and touched so as to make marks. These marks are supposed by those concerned to be like certain characters in their writing, and some kind of an answer is manufactured out of them. This is done after asking the gods to guide them. The room, which is about thirty by twenty feet, and up-stairs in a back court, is filled with all sorts of images of bronze and wood carving, and some really interesting things. A man to whom we were introduced pays 1,000 dollars a year for the place, and takes a certain charge from the worshippers and makes a good thing out of it. They burn candles and incense, and offer flowers to their gods, and the place has a

THE CHINESE QUARTER. 95

peculiar odour, but not very disagreeable. Below this is a meeting-house or committee-room, where the Chinaman in charge was not very civil.

We then went through some of the lowest and worst streets and alleys, some very filthy, and up into an opium-smoking establishment—a dirty loft with shelves for the smokers. A man in charge, in a sort of bed, prepares the opium by burning it in a lamp. It is quite an art, they say, and when cooked smells quite nice. The smoker then takes it and swallows all the smoke he can get from it, passing it out (after retaining it as long as possible) through his nose. The agreeable sensation comes on some time afterwards and leaves them in a sort of dream. There were twenty men I should think in this place, and all looked more dead than alive; none seemed to have enough energy to look at us even. The place smelt very strong. We paid a quarter of a dollar for the information and instruction, and were glad to get into the air. A more dreadful place it is almost impossible to conceive.

After this we went into a better sort of place, a really nicely fitted up café or tea-house, or whatever you may call it; so much better that we decided on having some tea and preserved fruit. For the latter we had chopsticks. The wood carving about this place was really interesting.

In a silversmith's we went into, we saw them working in a primitive way. Their light was from a sort of lamp made by putting oil into a saucer, the wick being a kind of grass, which was kept over the edge of the saucer in such a way that it formed a wick.

We then went into a lodging-house where there were several hundred of the lowest Chinese living, and where filth and vice seemed to be allowed to run mad. Then into a street given up entirely to gambling-dens, with men watching at every door to give the alarm in case of an officer of the law being in sight; when one appears the doors are closed and a stand is made. We were told that these dens are winked at, and that those who ought to prevent such places from being open take their weekly blackmail of the proprietors for leaving them in peace. Some of the courts and dens were fearful. That human creatures should be created to live such a life seems extraordinary. We saw more vice and depravity than I can possibly describe, and were pleased to get into a comparatively pure sort of place, and this was on the stage of one of their theatres. We went through their dressing, or what we should call green rooms—a filthy set of cellars very little higher than your head, where the smell was as strong as ever, and where the Chinese actors were in a state of dress or undress, as the case may be. These rooms were entered by passages so long, dark, low, and narrow, that it gave you a feeling of suffocation. We were introduced to and shook hands with the stage-manager, who seemed also to be chief performer, and who at the time was changing his costume and had nothing but his trousers on. We were accommodated with seats on the stage and spent best part of an hour watching the performance. It was a tragedy, and spoken in a kind of blank verse; between each line there was a crash of cymbals, and at certain parts, other instruments: a one-stringed fiddle and three trumpets, altogether a most fearful sound. There was no scenery: it was imagined. A door was pretended to be opened at the proper time, and in one part horses were supposed to have been brought in, and several of the characters mounted. We were told we must always consider the characters mounted when they had whips in their hands, of which there was a stock on the stage. They never allow women to go on the stage, but men dress up and paint like women, and really make up very well and imitate a woman's voice in their parts. The house was crowded. The women do not sit with the men, but in a gallery by themselves. We left by another set of private dens and underground passages, in some of which men were asleep. In this place there was a kind of a temple over the stage with the gods of the theatre in it, and we went up to see it, but at the time there were no worshippers.

We went into the private dwelling of the oldest Chinese inhabitant of the town : a room perhaps seven feet by ten, very low, with a bed in it. It was in a back court under the level of the road. The old man asked us in, but the stench was so fearful I could not get rid of it, and should have run out, but that I felt bound to give him something as I had so far intruded on him. I have never before spent such an evening. The worst Indian savage cannot be as badly down in the social scale as some of these people; there is an utter want of nobility about them. Those Indians we saw at St. Augustine's were splendid specimens of humanity compared with many we saw to-night.

The sights have almost upset me. I suppose the low parts of London may be bad; is it possible they can be anything like what we have seen to-night? I can only hope not quite so bad.

It is twelve and I must be off to bed. We intend to have another look at the Chinese quarter to-morrow by daylight.

12*th*.—On inquiry we found we could not get seats for the Yosemite Valley coach on Thursday, but could this afternoon, and so took them while we had the chance. The round trip, *i.e.* from San Francisco to Yosemite and back, is 50 dollars per head, which seems a very big price, but I think it is a pity not to see it. We started at 3.30, slept in the train, and got to a station called Raymond about six in the morning, had breakfast there, and took our seats on the coach for the first day's ride up the lower part of the Sierra Nevada mountains. It is a fertile slope covered with oak and small shrub trees, and game of all sorts. Although the distance is under forty miles it took us the whole day to travel the first stage, which was to a place called Clarke's Hotel, built in a pretty dent in the side of the mountain. We changed horses four times, and had to our coach sometimes four, once five, and once six, according to the steepness of the road. The farther we got on the way the larger the trees became and the more dangerous the roads. At last the trees were nearly all firs and some very large. Clarke's Hotel is a nice one. We were put up in a detached building which had twenty or thirty rooms on the ground floor, and we were comfortable, although very cold. We rose at five the next morning, had breakfast at six, and I had time for a little walk before the start. The sheep from the lowlands were being driven on to the mountains. The men in charge sleep out of doors alongside their sheep, and are armed against the wild animals, of which there are plenty about here. I was told if I liked to spend the night in the forest above where the sheep were sheltered, I was almost sure to get a shot or two either at bears or Californian lions, something like a panther, large animals whose weight averages about 130 lbs. However, whether it was from fatigue or whether

I thought perhaps the wild animals might have the best of it I cannot say, but I decided on going to bed, which I did. The drive from Clarke's on to the valley, twenty-six miles, is a most wonderful one; the road is too narrow and steep, and sometimes the wheels seemed to go too near the edge and the distance to fall was very great, but we arrived safe and sound in time for lunch. There is a place called Inspiration Point, where the valley first comes into view, and where you can form a very good idea of it. It is a tremendous gap cut by the river through granite mountains; the sides are in many places almost perpendicular. At one part a rock named El Capitan stands like a wall 3,300 feet high (more than half a mile)—you can hardly realise it. The fir-trees are enormous, many over 200 feet high, and yet they look as nothing against this rock. There was one fir, 150 feet high, standing on a little ledge part of the way up the rock; I was a long time before I could see it, it appeared to be so small.

The waterfalls from the tops of these clefts into the valley fall such a distance before they touch anything that although they are large streams, they are completely broken up into a kind of thick mist, and, if there is any wind, water the valley for some distance round. There are three of these splendid falls (beside many smaller) opposite the window of the room I am writing in. There are three little hotels here—rough but comfortable. Frank and I have walked about ten miles since we came here. We think of staying two days. We slept well last night, as we were very tired, and as we had to get up at half-past five to go to the Mirror Lake to see the sun rise, we went to bed early. Breakfasted at six, and reached the lake, three miles off, about seven, just in time. The mountains and trees are reflected in the lake most beautifully, and as the sun does not rise above the tops of the mountains for several hours after he is seen in other places, he is not visible here until past seven. As you look in the lake and he lights up the tops of the mountains, the effect is very beautiful and quite repaid us for our trouble. It is necessary, in order to obtain a full view of this extraordinary valley, to get on some high point, so that you can see the whole formation—the waterfalls and the surrounding mountains. The best point, we were told, was Glazier Point—in fact, this is the highest point accessible, and this only by a mule-path several miles in length cut in the rocks and having over fifty zigzags in it. As some others were going up this morning we joined them and hired some little horses and guides. It was a rare climb and a slip would have been serious, as in many places there was nothing to prevent a fall to the bottom. At first it was not nice to look down, but as we got higher that feeling went off, and we had more the feeling of being up in a balloon. We went up about four thousand feet above the valley, and the view from the top was glorious—the little river, green as grass, winding its way along the valley, and a full view of the enormous rocks that enclose it on every side. The trees, that looked from the bottom like small shrubs, were, when we were near them, 150 to 200 feet high, and from the top you could hardly distinguish the cattle in the valley. We threw some pieces of rock down, but lost all sight of them before they were a tenth part of the way to the bottom. I do not suppose there are any other cliffs so sheer upright, or falls that leap into the air and break up, first into silver, and then into spray, as these do here. How the valley has been formed I cannot make out; it seems almost impossible that such a river can have cut it, and if it has cut it, it must have taken millions of years.

There is very seldom any rain here, but a good depth of snow on the mountains. As we came down again a storm-cloud gathered and looked as if it would burst on us; but it did not, and it is now clear and the sun shining again.

The ride down seemed more dangerous than the climb up, as at some of the angles there seemed to be much too little room for the horses and mules to turn, and the great depth was always before us. I and one or two others walked and led our horses down the worst places, and we were all rather glad to get down, and were tired.

I forgot to mention that an enterprising man lives with his family on the top, and gave us a very good lunch and a bottle of Californian wine. I should like to stay here for some time; I have never seen a place where the same effects are produced. If you were an artist you might spend the summers of your life here. There are some nice mountain trout in the rivers and streams, and they cook them very well. They are caught by the Indians for the hotel.

The tribe of Yosemite Indians, never a very large one, has dwindled down to thirteen. They are living in three huts in the valley; they live on bread made of acorns prepared in a curious way, and other primitive food. I should say a few years would see the end of them. They are a very inferior race and have some strange customs. They burn their dead, and during the ceremony dance and make a great noise in order to attract the evil one's attention, that the heart may not be stolen by him, as they suppose that the heart passes into a future existence.

Wild animals, *i.e.* the large ones, seem to keep clear of the valley since it has been taken possession of by the whites; but there are plenty all round. Our guide tells us some very large bears have been killed on the mountains. The timber land round here can be bought of the Government for from $1\frac{1}{2}$ to $2\frac{1}{2}$ dollars per acre. The timber, if it could be marketed, would be valuable; but as it is it is useless and is being destroyed. The valley is reserved for the public, and will be some day visited by the million. The reservation extends for one mile round the cliffs, *i.e.* outside of them. In one place we passed there was to me a novel kind of conveyance for taking timber to market. A trough, fifty-six miles long, has been constructed of wood alongside a stream, and water enough turned into it to fill it and float timber, one log, or several boards at a time. As the trough is at a hanging level the water runs at about five miles an hour. The timber put in at the saw-mill at the upper end takes thirteen hours to do the journey, and of course there is a continuous succession of pieces floating down, so that it would convey an immense quantity. I understand this mode of conveyance is in existence in Norway, but I have never before seen it.

The gold-mining interest in California seems to be great. We passed one large gold mine, and trial holes have been sunk in various places. There are also several sulphur and other springs, so that I suppose what with its mineral wealth and climate it will some day be a well-populated country.

15*th, Sunday.*—Had a walk all round the valley. Started between eight and nine and did not get back to the hotel until lunch time. We miscalculated our distance, or should have gone to a service held in a little wooden church, conducted by a lady staying in one of the hotels. All who attended said she did it beautifully, and preached a most telling sermon; as it was, our sermon was one from the rocks, and a very impressive one too. The size and grandeur grew upon us. The trees at their feet, some 200 feet high, looked nothing against the vast mass of rock. All the morning, part was being lit up by the glorious sunshine and part thrown into deep shadow. The birds were of the brightest colours, and the butterflies three times the size of those at home, and the most beautiful I have ever seen; waterfalls, some taking a clear leap into space, their spray producing rainbows in the sunshine, altogether the scene was almost unnaturally beautiful. Another long walk in the evening finished our day. We started at six on Monday morning on our return journey, arrived at Clarke's Hotel to lunch, after a mountain drive of twenty-six miles, had an hour's rest, and started again for a journey and climb of 2,600 feet to the Mariposa grove of big trees.

All the trees about here are very large; but the Wellingtonias—the same as we have small specimens of in England—grow in one or two places to an enormous size. Where we went to-day there were about three hundred large ones and a great many smaller ones in a sheltered position on the mountain side. They are, I suppose, the largest trees in the world—many are 15 to 20 feet through the butt, and 200 to 250 feet high; but there are several specimens much larger—one 100 feet in circumference and nearly 300 feet high. We measured the circumference ourselves, and I measured the length of a fallen one and made it 260 feet; it had been down for years, and as the top was large, it must have been much taller. The highest specimen, they say, is 326 feet, or nearly half as high again as the Monument.

A carriage-road has been cut through the butt of one, and the section (I measured it) is 27 feet through. By counting the rings they make the ages of some of the largest trees to be three or four thousand years.

Whether this is right or not I cannot tell, but certain it is the trees are most wonderful in size.

The wood is of a darkish pink colour, and the trees themselves are not so beautiful as some of the other fir-trees, and are all more or less damaged by fire. One has the centre burned completely out—you can get inside and look up, as though you were looking up a very large chimney. This sort of fir only grows in one or two spots, and is quite different from any of the other kinds which surround it.

We shall sleep at Clarke's to-night, and go to bed early, as we have to start in good time to-morrow. The drive back to Raymond enabled us to see the view looking west on descending the mountains. The slopes below are not covered with fir-trees but oak and small shrubs, leaving room for herbage between, and look very beautiful, just like an immense park. In fact it would make a splendid preserve of unlimited extent, and I should think might be bought for a few shillings an acre, and used for that purpose and grazing to advantage, as the winters are not very severe on the western slopes, and there are many streams of good water.

We fell in with one of Raymond's excursion parties. He manages excursions as Cook does in England. They were rather a mixed lot, but a few were very superior, nice people. A Mr. Whiting, a molasses merchant of Boston, travelling with his wife and daughter, seemed to be very well-informed. I promised to send him out a photograph of the small Wellingtonias we have, as they do not seem to cultivate them in the States, and also to send him the particulars of the Willesden water-proof paper. Then there was a Mr. Jayne, a friend of his, who had travelled a good bit, a very nice man; a small lady of a lecturing turn of mind, who I should think could take the chair at a meeting called for the protection of woman's rights; an oldish lady who had lived principally in the train since January; and a married lady of the shady side of forty, who was full of fun, and many others. They were all particularly kind to us, and were constantly asking our opinions of the States and Americans generally. We joined their party back into 'Frisco, and had a private Pullman car. This little trip off the road is looked upon as a small one, but it involves four hundred miles of railway travelling, and nearly a hundred and fifty miles of staging over one of the most difficult roads I have seen.

18*th*.—We passed the remainder of the day in the city of San Francisco, walking again round the Chinese town, and looking into stores, &c. We spent part of the evening with our friends at the Palace Hotel, and were introduced to a Mr. Newton, of Holyoke, Mass., a young partner in a large paper-making firm. They have four mills, and make forty or fifty tons of paper a day. Delegates from the Young Men's Christian Associations, which are very numerous and powerful in the States, have a series of meetings at Oakland this year. Mr. Whiting attended to take part in the proceedings. He informed me the Association had, I think he said, 1,100 different branches, and 150,000 members; they do not work with any particular Church, but embrace the whole of the Christian denominations, and work independently of the clergy. They have very fine buildings in almost every town.

Next morning we had a ride to the higher part of San Francisco, and went to the station where the power is provided for the cable railways. It is splendidly arranged; they have two pairs of engines, 150 horsepower each pair, one pair being used as a stand-by in case of a breakdown. The cable is endless, working over grooved wheels, and as it expands and contracts in consequence of the alteration of the temperature of the weather, it is led over a grooved wheel placed on a trolly, having a weight to keep it extended to the necessary strain.

There is a machine for making the cable on the spot. The cable is a little over an inch in diameter, made over a core of Manilla rope. They can put a new cable on to the works for the whole length of several miles in an hour and a half, by splicing the new to the old, and leading the old off on to some spare drums. I was pleased to find the best wire could be got from Gateshead, England, and that they were using it, although more expensive, in consequence of the duty; it stood the work better, and the cable now running is made of it. They have 150 tons of the Gateshead wire on the way out.

These cable tramways are an undoubted success out here; they run up and down the steepest hill with perfect safety, can be stopped and started with ease, and pay well. It has altogether passed beyond the stage of experiment; they are being put down everywhere. The climate of this place is not satisfactory: it is cold and damp, there is almost always a fog hanging over the town, and although the variation of the temperature is not great between summer and winter, it is certainly not the place for invalids. In the afternoon we started on our trip to Portland, Oregon. It is about 800 miles off, and getting there takes forty-eight hours, as part of it has to be done by stage coach. The land is for a long distance flat between the mountains, and seems to be very good for agriculture. This is one of the largest wheat-producing states of the Union, and the wheat grown here fetches the highest price in the English market. We slept on the car, and in the morning arrived at the end of the rail, the last few miles being over an unfinished road, very uneven, and with temporary bridges, over the streams. The country is wooded and beautiful, and the railway runs up the sides of the mountains in splendid style. The rivers, they say, are full of fish. After great trouble the passengers were packed into three of the regular old American coaches. Our baggage had to be left behind, as there was no room for it, and we commenced the roughest ride by far I have ever had. The road, or rather track, was entirely without hard material of any kind, and the ruts so deep, we were in constant danger of turning over. We had to ford the streams, and only progressed over part of the road at the rate of two miles an hour. In fact, we had to walk very often. In one case the coach stuck fast going down a steep hill; although we had six horses the wheels sunk in so far they could not go round, and we had to clear out the passengers before it could be got out. In some places small trees and branches were laid over the road. We had no springs but leather, and the shaking and cramping was dreadful. We, however, came through a delightful country, first over the northern spurs of the Sierra Nevada, and then along the Umpqua river and the middle of the coast range of mountains, having Mount Shasta and the Cascade Mountains in sight. At one little shanty a very old black man, whose hair was perfectly white, gave us some splendid hashed venison; although it ought not to have been shot at this season of the year, it was very good. We got to Ashland late, but the train waited for us, and we are now comfortably installed in a Pullman car again, having had our dinner, and the beds are just being made up. The fields are green and full of crops and cattle. Except for the winters, I should prefer this part of the country to most others I have seen.

21*st*.—We arrived in Portland at 10 A.M., and put up at the Esmond Hotel, the largest hotel having just been burned down. Our yesterday's drive and rail ride was all through Oregon Territory, and a splendid district it is. Portland is a very nice business city on the Willamette River. There are some very fine stores here, and at the back there are capital residences with good well-kept gardens. The people are not so much in a hurry as those in most of the other cities, and seem contented and well-to-do. We turned the hotel register back some distance, but could not find a name from England. As there is splendid fishing, shooting, and scenery, I wonder more do not come. There are two beautiful mountains— extinct volcanoes—Mount Hood and Mount St. Helen—in sight, covered with snow a long way down. The river is a very fine one; any-sized vessel almost can get up here. Several English vessels are now taking in timber, as this is one of the greatest timber-producing States. The lumbering, *i.e.* cutting timber, is a big trade. A district is purchased and a regular lumbering gang formed, usually about 150 hands; a tram is laid down one of the valleys to the nearest stream to bring the timber down, and a small winding engine is used to pull the logs to the trams. The trees are cut off about six feet from the ground (timber is so plentiful they do not mind how much they waste). It is then cross-cut into the desired lengths; one man does this, even for the largest logs, and they are sent down to the mill, usually on the creek. The men get $1\frac{1}{4}$ dollars a day and their food; the foreman this year 85 dollars a month. The cook of the camp is an important personage and well paid. The men are a rough lot, work ten hours a day, and gamble and sleep away the rest of the time. A tree six feet through and 200 feet high is not at all an unusual size.

Washington Territory is just over the Columbia River. We are trying to arrange to go to Puget Sound and to Vancouver Island, but we must draw the line somewhere, or we shall not be back in New York in time to catch our boat. Highway robbery has not altogether ceased here yet. We were shown the remains of some mail-bags taken from a stage some little time ago, just on the brow of a hill; and on one of our stages, when they were carrying some bullion, there was a man placed with a double-barrelled gun on the box and another behind to protect it, as there had been several robberies within a little time. The labour on the coast is done in a great measure by Chinese. The railway in course of construction to cover the country over which we last drove was being made entirely by them. There were several thousands of them in camps in different places. They get about a dollar a day and their food, but work slowly. They make curious ovens in the earth for cooking their food, and seem easily managed. Not far from our road was a large vineyard of over two thousand acres, getting into good order. The Californian wines are, I think, very good, and will come into the market shortly. The best, I think, is a kind of claret, but they also make a fair white wine and champagne. The street cars here, as at some other places, are driven by a man who also acts as conductor, and has no help. You have to put the fare into a box yourself as you get in.

22nd.—We went to one of the prettiest little wooden churches I have ever seen. It was made of Californian red wood and the white pine, mingled in such a way as to be very ornamental. The mouldings and all interior fittings were of wood, as also was the ceiling. I should think something might be done in this way, *i.e.* mingling the woods of different colours, in England. As we passed the St. Charles Hotel, we heard the fire-alarm given, as there was a fire on the back premises. We timed the fire-engines,

&c. The reel of hose was on the spot in one minute, the fire-escape and ladders in under two minutes, and two steam fire-engines in under four minutes, and they were pumping almost immediately afterwards. This seems to me good work; the engine-house was, however, close by. The Columbia River is, I find, some distance down. The Willamette is a very beautiful stream, with plenty of fish in it. We shall see the Columbia to-morrow. There is a bridge over the river here constructed very cheaply. Part of it swings to let vessels through, and although the piece swinging is 308 feet long, it is so nicely balanced it is moved easily by one man; it is balanced on a pivot in the centre, and turned like a turntable. The young fellow at the desk in the hotel here is the son of a man in good position in Edinburgh, and has been educated as a doctor—a most gentlemanly young fellow. He says he brought a little money out, but lost it in mining speculations. He has driven a coach, and been so hard up that he has only had two meals in three days; but he says he likes the place, and thinks he shall now get on. His case is that of many thousands. You need not feel at all surprised if you find that the man blacking your boots is much better educated and better informed than yourself. I have found that out already several times.

23*rd.*—Our journey to-day was at first for forty miles down the Columbia River, one of the finest streams, I suppose, in the world; it drains a district as large as France and Germany, and that, too, where there is continual snow on the mountains. The land by the side has been turned into water meadows, where the high bank and timber is sufficiently far back. The train was taken over the Columbia River on one of the large ferry-boats. The operation occupied about three-quarters of an hour, during which time a very good lunch was served in a dining-room on board the ferry-boat for half a dollar; the food was well cooked, and the room nicely decorated with flowers. We then had a five hours' ride through Washington Territory to a place called Tracona. The country we passed through was partly cleared, and had some very nice streams through it. Tracona is at the southernmost point of Puget Sound, and will, I suppose, be made into an important port and a watering-place; but the shore is very flat just here, and the tide when out leaves a large space uncovered, which is a very great drawback. The mountain—now called Tracona, after the town, which stands some distance behind—you can see from every point; it looks very beautiful; we could see the outline even when it was nearly dark. We went on board the steamer and took our berths, as she sails at 4 in the morning, and then went to have a look at the large hotel, a well-built brick building of considerable size and well-found. We were very much amused by an advertising gang, who had a kind of music-hall platform fitted upon wheels, and drawn by two grey horses. A well-dressed woman played the harmonium, and the three men had good voices, and sang a good selection of semicomic songs. Between each, one of the men made a humorous speech, puffing his patent medicines, and his wit was extraordinary; he turned any chaff he received to account at once. He would have done for an Irish member. The whole party were staying at one of the best hotels.

24th.—Got up between five and six to see as much as possible of Puget Sound. It is a splendid piece of water, something like the Solent, but much more extensive, and having all sorts of islands and headlands in it, nicely wooded, with snow-clad mountains behind. There are some good towns on the shore; one, Seattle, we called at; it has some fine school and other buildings, and seems to be a good place for trade. The next was Port Townsend, where we had time to land and walk round. There are collieries here, and conveniences for loading a 2,500-ton steamer in twelve hours. We then had a thirty-five-mile steam over a large piece of water, Strait of Juan de Fuca, open at one point to the Pacific and consequently a little rough, but of a splendid colour. The mountains of the coast range could be seen at several points above the clouds and looked very strange. We got to Victoria, Vancouver Island, about 3.30. As this was the first Canadian port, and as there were three English men-of-war here, it looked very homelike, and the people much more like ourselves—English carriages, and dog-carts, and other things; but the place has less life about it than the States' towns. The Island of Vancouver is in many respects like Great Britain; it is about the same distance from mainland as England is from France. The climate and vegetation is very much like that of the south of England, with a fair amount of rain, and very little snow and frost. The roads are made as we make ours, and good. The island is about 300 miles long and something under 100 miles wide; but the population is at present very small, 7,500. I looked in at a land agent's; he had a farm of 1,760 acres (600 acres cleared and cultivated) he asked £1,760 for, or 5 dollars an acre. Another of 600 acres for 3 dollars, or

12s., an acre; and a little shooting-box on sixty acres of land and boat-house, with water frontage, for £200. I dare say he would have taken less. This gives some idea of values.

There are very good coal mines here yielding a considerable quantity. I made the acquaintance of the owner; he said he had to raise it about 300 feet, and sent 1,500 tons a month to San Francisco alone. He surprised me by telling me a considerable amount of coal came from England to San Francisco. This island should be better known; it would be just the place for Englishmen to settle in, if they could only get here.

The railways of the States are doing all they can to injure the Canadian Pacific Railway. They will not grant through tickets over it from any of their western cities. I arranged a through rate with the agent at Portland from Portland to Winnipeg, but had to get money enough returned out of the rate to pay our fare to this place, as the companies working up to here will not let the Canadian Pacific people handle any of the money, although they grant through rates over each others' lines all over the States. I am writing this rather late at night on board a very fine steamer, which is to sail during the night for Vancouver, *i.e.* the town, which is on the mainland. It is the largest we have been on, and makes up a number of berths. There are several people about the cabins talking before they turn into bed. In the morning we found we had got a considerable distance on our way, and were in sight of the mountains surrounding the new town of Vancouver. The entrance to the harbour is between high hills covered with timber and very narrow. When you are in, it is a most beautiful and convenient harbour, with water for any sized vessels, and as this is the western port of the Canadian Pacific Railway, I suppose it is destined to be one of the great ports of the western coast. Nothing could be more protected, more convenient, or more picturesque. There was a small place on the spot before the construction of the railway, but it was cleared off by fire eleven months

VANCOUVER.

ago in thirty minutes. The fire got hold of the forest, which was very dense, and simply licked the small town of wooden houses out of existence. The people ran for their lives to any spare space, and chiefly into the water, but many were burned. The exact number is not known. This place is now laid out as a large town, and if ever built as designed, will be as big as some of the large eastern cities of the States. There are at present wide streets paved with planks, and with plank side walks, and some very tidy houses, several built of brick and stone, and it is, for the time it has been in existence, a wonderful place. The stumps of the trees left by the fire are still standing all round, and a more extraordinary sight you cannot imagine. They must have stood very thick indeed, and been very large. This is another place where a young man with a little money and brains could get on well. It simply must go ahead, it has everything that is necessary to create a large port and place of business. We met a gentleman, a clergyman, here we crossed the Atlantic with, and when we were in a shanty buying a photograph a young man walked in who was in the Cunard office in London when I got my tickets. He said he remembered my face again, and asked if we were going back to England, and, on being told we were, begged Frank to call on his parents at Catford Bridge to tell them we had seen him. Frank was to be sure to drop in just at dinner-time on them, which he promised to do. This young fellow was on the Stock Exchange, but is now in a surveying party for the railway company. We spent the morning in going over a large saw-mill; the mill was home-made and old, but some of the contrivances were very good. All the work was done on a floor about fifteen feet from the ground. The logs were floated up to one end of the mill, and drawn on to the platform by means of an endless chain having very large links set in motion at pleasure by pressing a pulley on to a loose band, same as we make small lifts at home, a smaller chain being attached to the timber and hooked into one of the links of the large chain. The log was then placed on a bench on which there were two circular saws, one working over the other, so that where the bottom saw was not deep enough to go through the cut, the other one came in and helped. It cut through a log twenty feet long in thirty seconds. The log was canted as required by means of another chain with a hook on end, and fixed to a pulley overhead, also worked by pressure gearing, and very easily. When the stuff was planked, it passed on to another sawbench further ahead and was edged; then it was pushed along rollers into a vessel waiting for cargo. The mill was turning out cut timber as fast as the vessel could be loaded with it. The boilers were kept going by the sawdust, which was conveyed from the different places by pieces of board 3 inches by 6 inches by 1 inch, drawn along the bottom of a wooden box, on an endless chain or wire. When the loaded pieces of board got in front of the boiler-furnace the sawdust was swept off by means of pieces of leather hanging down and left exactly where it was wanted.

They have circular saws out here with teeth made to take in and out, so that when a saw wants sharpening you put in a fresh set of teeth, which can be done in a short time; but they cut away an immense quantity of stuff, waste of timber being of no consequence. The best timber boards are sold at 15 dollars per thousand superficial feet, 1 inch thick, which is the standard all cut lumber, as they call it, is sold by. We are now passing up alongside the Fraser River, the best fish stream in the world. The salmon are so thick at some seasons of the year they stop boats going up. This sounds too much, but it is told me by a most sober Canadian, and not by a Californian. The information given by the latter is generally doubted, but I don't like to begin to doubt the Canadians already. However, there is no doubt the river, which is an immense one, is very full of fish, and the trade done in tinned salmon is one of the leading industries of the district. It is also true that a twenty-pound salmon can be got for a few pence. The Indians are very numerous here, but seem to work. There is a Roman Catholic mission for Indians on the opposite shore to Vancouver. The little settlement is clean and pretty. I bought a picture of it.

The station at Vancouver was only opened yesterday by the directors, on the Queen's birthday, and this is the first train out. We are therefore the first passengers. They made a bit of a fuss. There are triumphal arches of evergreens and the remains of yesterday's decorations. Most of the men have sleepy eyes, as if they had lived freely yesterday. The train was consequently a little late in starting. A farmer I asked as to the climate tells me it is quite mild here up to the Rocky Mountains. It is just like England, with perhaps a little more wet. The greatest objection is that the woods in summer are always burning, and for weeks together whole districts are enveloped in a yellow, pitchy-smelling smoke; but that will cure itself, as if they persevere there will some day be no more beautiful timber to burn. They have a curious arrangement here for unloading railway trucks loaded with mould. The trucks are simply platforms made to project at the ends, so that they form a continuous floor; the mould is piled up on this, and there is a kind of plough, made of wood shod with iron at the end furthest from the engine; the plough is made so as to throw the stuff off each side, and when the trucks are blocked the plough is attached by a chain to the engine and drawn forward, and it clears all the trucks of their load in a minute or two. The truck with the plough on is then shunted to rear of the train and the operation can be repeated. The plough is kept from leaving the trucks by two guides, one hanging over each side.

We are climbing up by the side of the Fraser River on a road cut in the rocks alongside. It is a beautiful river, narrowing between high rocks as we get up it, with here and there a rock in the middle trying to stop the water from flowing down, but only with the result of heading it back and making the rushing torrent more beautiful. The railway in some places is on a doubtful foundation, as clay is mixed with the rocks, and when it is disturbed the clay washes away and the rocks tumble over. The snows are melting, so that the railway traffic has to be carried on with the greatest care. The train due Friday last was two days behind time, and the train to the west to-day is seventeen hours behind. We, however, seem to be keeping time so far.

We dined at a little hotel put up by the company on the side of the mountain. The hotel is very tastily built of wood, and the food good. The next morning found us on the lower east side of Coast Mountains, by the side of a splendid lake surrounded by the fir-clad mountains of the Gold Range. The lake is very much like some of the Scotch lakes, and full of fish and wild-fowl. More mountain climbing led us to what is called the Divide Lake, water at one end running out to Fraser River and the other to a branch of the Columbia River. We had our breakfast car with us. This is very well found and fitted: ferns on the table, and good food and attendance for 75 cents, or 3s., a head. All up the Fraser River men seem to go in for gold washing on their own account, *i.e.* two or three working together washing the sand brought down by the melting snows. They must get some gold or so many would not be at it.

The forest fires have literally devastated a good bit of the country alongside the railway about here, and spoiled its beauty. Nothing but charred remains of trees, mostly on the ground but many standing, like blackened spectres. The destruction is awful. All parties seem to combine to destroy; timber being treated as an enemy everywhere, and destruction carried on where it cannot possibly have an excuse. Not one forest fire, but hundreds are now burning. We are scarcely ever out of sight of one, although they do not at this time of the year assume large proportions.

We, at about nine o'clock, began to ascend by the side of a branch of the Columbia River, or rather of a mountain river running into the Columbia, through a beautiful valley to the Albert Cañon, which is not so dark or deep as that passed on the Rio Grande, but still very grand and beautiful. They allow you on the trains to run about as you like, and to stand on the outside platforms, no matter how dangerous the places are. It makes the time pass more quickly. As I am writing the train has just brought up for a rock ahead, one having slipped down on to the track. We are in a pretty spot, the water dashing down from the mountain and sparkling in the sunshine. This obstruction is scarcely removed before we have news of another landslip, or rather rockslip, further in front, and have taken aboard some men and dynamite so that we may clear our way. The train ran on a mile or two until she got to the obstruction. We have walked over a river bridge and through a snow-shoot to see what it is. It is not very serious. A couple of charges has broken it up sufficiently to allow the men to remove it. In the broken rock there are pieces containing lead and silver, and something resembling gold but much lighter. We got some specimens. They say we shall have all clear in two or three hours. We are to lunch about ten miles further ahead if we can get there. Our breakfast car left us to tack on to a train going the other way to provide the passengers with lunch. The snow has slid down from the mountains on to the stream and has bridged it over in several places, the water having cut holes and made large snow arches. There are, they say, about thirty snow-shoots or sheds on these mountains, all very well constructed. As soon as the slip was cleared and we started on our journey we were brought up by a heavy freight train coming down the other way, and as there are no sidings except at points some miles distant each way, considerable delay was caused in settling which should go back. The passenger train has the right of the road, but the freight train is very heavy, and although she has two engines can hardly get up the hill. However, it is settled she is to try, and there is now a kind of procession of trains climbing the mountain at walking pace. We are all getting hungry, as it is past lunch time, and our lunch-station is some distance ahead. There must have been something wrong to allow two trains running in opposite directions to get on the single line together, and the landslip may have served us a good purpose. After several stoppages we managed to get by at the siding, but the road was so bad and had been washed away by the melting snow in so many places we were two hours more in getting to the Glacier Hotel, which is nearly at the top of the pass of the Selkirk Range. This range seems to be more difficult to get over than any of the others. We had our midday meal here some hours late, and it was, in consequence, rather overdone but extraordinarily good for such a place, as everything around was buried in snow. Just here a train is buried and has been there since February, when the snow came down and wrecked it, killing several men. They are digging it out. It was completely smashed, and was covered up with snow, trees, and stones brought down by the sliding snow. Our difficulties were not over, however. On starting again the road was found to be bad, the foundation having been washed away, and then a rock of some tons weight had got on to the road, which had to be broken up and removed. In many places timber had been put under the road into the bank, the outer end being propped up from the rock below. The road was so uneven the carriages lurched, sometimes dangerously. However, at last we reached the highest part. On crossing the ridge the water began to run with us, so that we knew we were over the pass. Altogether there are miles of beautifully constructed snow-sheds and immense cuttings through snow. In some cuttings there was a spare line of rails, so that the men might have a better chance of keeping one clear. We passed over some very fine tressel-bridges, one 280 feet high and another 1,100 feet long and 170 feet high, with 1,250,000 feet of timber in it. There were many landslips on this side, but nothing to stop us. Lower down there was a valley not unlike the Yosemite, having about such another river running through it, but the mountains round were not so high or so steep, and no large waterfalls. There we hit the Columbia River again, which takes a very strange bend north, and is here, as elsewhere, a beautiful stream. The railway company lost several cars here last year, consumed in a forest fire. The anxiety in running this line must be great, as from hour to hour something seems to happen to make parts unsafe. Some of the bridges over the river have been carried away by the sliding snow four times already. They are, however, gradually getting everything more safe; and as they find out the tricks of the snow and shifting rocks in different places, are able to make some provision against them.

We got down to a place called Donald, on the low land between the Selkirk and Rocky Mountains. This is the only place the company could find flat enough to build engine-sheds, &c., and they have formed a sort of colony here, and as it is completely buried in the mountains, and the men are cut off from civilisation, it is about the roughest place we have seen, and I should think resembles a mining camp. Some young Englishman belonging to a good family who had gone to the bad and was out here, was shot in a gambling saloon a few nights ago. We now began to ascend the Rockies. Here they are not so difficult to cross as they were further south; there are no difficult places or snow-sheds. Although we had to climb steep grades, with two engines, and pass through the usual cañon by the side of the river on entering (it was still a branch of the Columbia), we got on easily and had no further adventures. The Beaver River, where the Hudson Bay Company used to get so many skins for hat-making in times gone by, is here; in fact this is part of the district over which that Company held sway. I previously thought their territory was confined entirely to snow-covered districts, but it, in fact, includes large districts as fertile as England, with a similar climate. They have still a large share of the land, which they are selling as they can find a market for it.

27*th*.—The morning found us down on the prairie, with nothing but rolling grass lands as far as the eye can reach; they say it extends 1,000 miles from here, and although it looks fresh and green we shall soon tire of it. The Indians (here a finer set of men than many we have seen, clothed in whitish sort of cloaks) are now and then seen galloping over the plains on their ponies. We have taken a dining-car on, which is to accompany us until we get into inhabited parts again, and have just had breakfast served in an elegantly furnished dining-room. We had fruit, fresh fish nicely cooked, oatmeal porridge and cream, buttered toast and eggs, and could have had many more dishes if we had wanted them, and as much ice and fruit as we liked. The tables are very beautifully set out; cost of meal 75 cents, or say 3s. The silver is as bright as possible. At the end of the car a sideboard is set out with wines, vases, and flowers. This is a curious mixture of roughness and luxury. Indians as nearly wild, and without clothes or proper food, as you can imagine, living almost like animals, look in at the windows of Pullman drawing-room and dining cars, filled with every convenience the ingenuity of man can devise, and decorated in an absolutely artistic manner, regardless of cost. These cars cost the company £3,000 each, but six new ones they have just had built they say are altogether more costly and beautiful; the sleeping berths are as comfortable as a four-post bed at home, but the necessary curtains make them a little close, and when ladies are in the car the greater part of the dressing has to be done inside the berth, which is, until you get used to it, difficult. How the ladies can manage as they do is a marvel. They come out looking as fresh as daisies. At one end of the car there is a retiring room for the ladies, with every convenience, and at the other, one for gentlemen. I have shaved aboard every morning; the washing arrangements are capital; two can wash at a time. There is a nice smoking-room for gentlemen, and also a drawing-room for general use. One of the men has just shot a lynx at the last station; it seems to be a young one, like a very large cat, with extra-strong hind legs and claws. They have brought it on to the train; I should like to have it stuffed. The prairie is like the Atlantic after a storm, when the wind has gone down, leaving heavy rolling swells. Every now and then you can see for miles and miles, the distance looking just like water; and then you get down into a little hollow, where the roll nearest you takes off all view, as it does when you get into the trough of a sea. We have just passed "Medicine Hat," a settlement on the banks of a branch of the Saskatchewan river, which is navigable up to this place from some rapids lower down, small steamers having been built up here to ply on it. We are now in Assiniboine, having left Alberta early in the morning. We have just had dinner in the dining-car, served as well as it could be in a well-managed house. We had good soups, white fish from the Pacific, 1,200 miles away; salmon from the Columbia river; lamb and green peas; boiled mutton and caper sauce; beef; three made dishes; three sorts of pastry; fruit, oranges, and apricots from California, good cup of tea, plenty of ice, for 75 cents, or 3s. We had some good claret, 50 cents half bottle. This, so far from the base of supplies, is uncommonly good. The only drawback is that the coloured conductor, or rather porter, to the Pullman car, is a lazy, dirty fellow; but I

THE DINING CAR. 147

have blown him up and made him better. There are very few passengers in this car, but there are seven other cars of different kinds on the train, and in all, I suppose, seventy to one hundred passengers, some returning from Australia this way. When the line is finished over the mountains, which it will be when the nineteen miles of extra snow-sheds are completed, it will be the best and quickest way from ocean to ocean. The way all difficulties are tackled and overcome makes me think that it will be a good paying line some day, as no trouble is spared to serve passengers properly.

This district was formerly the great field for buffalo; they were here in enormous herds, so numerous that even now the collection of their bones for manure forms a large industry. We saw a large heap of them at one of the stations, and quite a gang of men with waggons and horses employed in the trade. The bones are worth 15 dollars a ton here, and cost another 15 dollars a ton for carriage into agricultural districts.

There are no buffaloes to be seen now, all having been destroyed for their skins, which fetched only 1 dollar, 4s., each. A few are found farther north, and one small herd is living under protection near the Yellowstone Park. They are trying to get them to breed with ordinary cattle, as their skins are good; it is therefore possible some of their blood may be saved in this way.

The Indians bring buffalo horns polished up for sale to almost every station; the horns are quite small for such large animals. I have bought a pair for 50 cents, or 2s. There is much more water than I expected to find; small lakes or large ponds are plentiful, and all of them have lots of wild-fowl on them. We are told any quantity can be shot in the season; it is now their breeding-time; there are several different sorts, and wild geese. Here the Indians have rugs of bright colours over their shoulders, and the women have their legs and feet bound round with a kind of scarlet cloth. They have very wide faces; they paint their foreheads and chins red, leaving the middle of their faces the natural colour. They do not seem to be able to understand much English, but are quite friendly. It would be safe to employ them on a hunting expedition.

We have just had our evening meal in the dining-car ; it is called tea, but good enough for dinner, as well cooked and served as the other meals have been. The car leaves us to-night and goes back to feed another train going west; in the morning we pick up another. The line is worked in twelve sections, a kind of sub-superintendent being in charge of each, and he seems to arrange by telegraph where the different trains are to shunt. I wonder they can do so well on a single line, as there are several trains running each way, and we are now running thirty-five miles an hour to pick up time lost on the mountains.

I am informed that prairie land can be rented of the Government at 2 cents, or 1d., per acre per year on lease for grazing purposes, and got in any desired quantity in any position not taken up, as it extends for something like a thousand miles from east to west, and perhaps as many from north to south ; there is plenty of choice.

We have just passed a lake called Rush Lake, literally covered with wild-fowl; they looked almost like flies on a fly-catcher. There are numbers on every little pool. We have also seen a prairie-wolf, but not much cattle and no sheep. We had a view of the Aurora Borealis, which is constantly seen here at night.

In the night we ran through the remainder of the perfectly open prairie, and came on to a district where large patches were cultivated with corn. It appears the way this is managed is that small owners cultivate as much as they can by their own strength and by the little labour they can command, growing chiefly wheat. They sell to men who have small elevators (warehouses), holding on an average 25,000 bushels of wheat, at the nearest station. The elevator-owners are the shippers or millers, and when they have bought enough at any place to make a consignment to the mill or for shipping, they draw it down spouts into the railway trucks and send it away. The settlers are extending farther west every year, leaving the ground they have exhausted and taking fresh; but as there is such an immense field this process may go on for a long time. The land through here is, I am told, almost exactly like that in the north of the United States. It is not very good, and produces what we in England would call a small crop, twenty bushels to the acre; it takes eight or ten acres to support each head of cattle, *i.e.* the average of it; of course there are spots where it is better than in the northern states. The climate, although farther north, is not colder. There seems to be less difficulty as to water here than farther south. I should fancy a man would do as well to come here as into the northern states of the Union.

An elevator to hold 25,000 bushels, with a small engine to hoist the grain, costs on the average 7,000 dollars, or say £1,400;

they are neat little places, and take up but little room.

This district is beginning to have patches of scrub wood on it, and the settlers' houses are more numerous, but they are terribly lightly built of wood, and how they can exist in them during the winter I do not know.

Land is to be bought of the Government and the Hudson Bay Company at $2\frac{1}{2}$ dollars per acre, with certain allowances, amounting to $1\frac{1}{4}$ dollar, for improvements if made.

The import duties of Canada average about 25 per cent. on invoice price. Almost everything pays duty, even to plants, young fruit-trees, seeds, and other things absolutely necessary for the development of the country; for instance, seedling fruit-trees, 20 per cent.; flower seeds 15 per cent., some 20 per cent.; while spades and ploughs pay 35 per cent., and works of art and things calculated to improve the taste and add to the enjoyment of the colonists pay 35 per cent. There is, however, a provision that paintings by Old Masters may be exempted.

Paper pays from 25 per cent. to 30 per cent.

I understand there is law against the export of waterfowl or game, although there is such an immense quantity of it. I should have thought, with a close season, an export trade in it might be allowed. The Customs tariff seems to be directed against the United States more than against any other country. There does not appear to be the best feeling between the two countries (Canada and the States), although I should fancy the interests of both would be better served by free intercommunication. In case of a fall out, the States are so much the stronger, and Canada has such a very extended frontier, she is bound, even with the assistance of the mother-country, I fear to get the worst of it, although I really do hope and think, from what I have seen and the good feeling generally expressed in the States towards the old country, it will be most easy to keep on good terms, and it would be a great pity if Canada should do anything to upset that good feeling. If England, her colonies, and the United States can agree and have a good understanding, their united influence in the affairs of the world will be strong indeed, and with a determination to keep command of the sea at any cost, can continue to do more for progress, free institutions, and civilisation than all the rest of the world together.

I cannot help thinking the Government of the States should be very closely watched and studied by our statesmen. The States are in themselves in some respects too free, and laws are being and will have to be passed to override the individual States in some instances. The Inter-State Commerce Law is an instance of this, and as the country gets more thickly populated other matters must be dealt with in the same way; but at the same time most of the powers now left with the States Governments may remain, and I think the time is not far distant when we in England will confer local powers on county boards something resembling what will ultimately be left to the different States of America, and that very many matters now occupying the time of our Parliament will be dealt with by these boards, and that in fact only the more important matters will be left to the House of Commons.

The Irish question is perhaps only the beginning of a much larger one, one that will lead up to the local self-government of the different parts of the United Kingdom and also influence the future of our colonies.

As we near Winnipeg we are taking some of the farming aristocracy into the train. They resemble our country gentlemen in dress and get up; they talk with a great deal of manner, and are evidently the society of the place, different to anything we have seen in the States, where equality is the order of the day. They talk of their balls, dinners, &c., and rather look down on common people. I should say the Canadians are a rather Conservative set of people, and cling to old ways perhaps a little too much.

Even the Indians are superior as you get

East. I have seen some quite swells, and one with a fairly good moustache.

Five o'clock brought us to Winnipeg, the advanced western town of Canada, corresponding to Kansas City and Omaha in the States, but not so lively. It is built on a perfectly flat plain having a clay soil, and although the streets are well laid out and wide, and the main street is paved with round blocks of wood, and has tramcar lines down it, the houses are not yet numerous enough to cover the sides. The corners of the different blocks have been covered with large brick buildings, stores, shops, &c., some very well built, and there are several very good churches. The climate is bad, I should think, as vegetation is very backward, and no fruit will grow here. This is one of the Hudson Bay Company's stations. They have a large store here, as they have in most of the large places, but I should think modern enterprise would cut them out, as they will not go into new ways, and until lately did not put their names up or give any indication that business could be done.

I saw maps showing the land they have for sale, an enormous quantity, which some day must be valuable. We slept the night here at the Leland Hotel, and started this morning (28th) for St. Paul, through the flattest and most uninteresting country possible, but here and there cultivated with corn. At Emmerson, the boundary between the two countries, our baggage was passed. There is at present nothing on this road worthy of note.

May 29th.—On the train from Winnipeg to St. Paul we met a very intelligent Scotch farmer, who had been in the States thirty-seven years. He farms a large farm south of St. Paul, which he said had now nearly worked itself out by continual wheat crops, and he had just bought a section, 640 acres, on the northern border of Minnesota, which he cropped entirely with wheat. He said he and his four sons did most of the work; that they ploughed with four horses eleven hours a day, turning a 14-inch furrow; that in the flat country there was nothing to hinder the cultivation. They never hoed the wheat, and in fact did nothing but roll it until harvest, when he had to pay men 8s. a day; but that he got good work out of them for this, as they had to move with the machines, which were driven by members of his family. They use light horses, as they walk so much faster. As a rule they thresh and market their wheat as soon as possible. It is now worth about 80 cents a bushel (26s. a quarter), delivered to the nearest elevator. He said also, hardly anything but wheat is grown about here, as it is too cold for Indian corn. The land costs but little; they have no tithes, and very little to pay for taxes, and they can just do at present prices, although it is not good work. I suppose, therefore, this is what the English farmers have to contend with. I will get cost of railway and ship freight to an English port if I can.

St. Paul is a fine city, well situated, with

high land on each bank of the river, but enough flat along the shore to leave room for business property. The country round is well cultivated; in fact, almost as well as one of the home counties of England. It is not a great manufacturing town, but I suppose has a large trading business as the centre of a fine agricultural district. The buildings are very large in some cases, and the foundations have to be piled, as it is on a sand. The bridges over the Mississippi are high up and useful, but not beautiful. The roads are paved in most cases with round wood blocks. This hotel, the Ryan, is built by a man who made a very large fortune in California in mining, and is now spending it in blocks of buildings in this city. He must be a man of considerable judgment and very rich, as it is splendidly built and very well managed by himself. The portion he has built cost £150,000, and the size is now being doubled.

There are some fine residences and roads on the high ground, some of the roads paved with asphalte; and electric light everywhere.

This is Decoration or Commemoration Day, set apart for decorating the graves of those who fell in the slave war. There was a funny kind of procession, each member dressing and marching as he thought best, and then some carriages filled with girls dressed as soldiers. They all went to the Town Hall, before which there was a platform erected, and a mixed entertainment given : prayers, speeches, music, recitations and singing, one recitation by a lady.

Just as the most important part was coming off, the floor of the platform gave way, and about one-third of those on it fell through, but as they only had about six feet to fall no one was much hurt. This incident, combined with a heavy shower of rain, rather spoiled the effect of the meeting.

The old farmer told me they had a machine to press the straw into compact bundles, so that they could send it by rail to the towns where much of it is used for paper-making and other purposes. It costs not quite 2 dollars, or 8 shillings, a ton to do it at the high price for labour they pay here.

31st.—Went to Minneapolis this morning. It is a very well built, fine city, and increasing very fast. There were 30,000 immigrants to it last year. The buildings are almost all stone and brick, and the streets well paved. The chief source of wealth is the power given by the river Mississippi here, as there are falls of 50 feet and an immense volume of water. The falls have been lined over with wood to keep the rock from wearing away, as it is soft; and the water is led, part of it at least, into channels by the side, and turbine-wheels fixed, producing an enormous power altogether, but still not half of it is utilised. The Knights of Labour have just begun to build a trade hall at Minneapolis. There is great fear here that they will run up labour too high, and injure the trade of the country. Labour is at present very unmanageable, but a good feature in it is, that when men do work they work well, and do not skulk, as some of our English mechanics do. We went over one large flour-mill, Pillsbury's. It is a sample of what enterprise will do. The power is derived from two turbine wheels, 54 inches diameter and 4 feet deep, with a head of water of 50 feet. This they say gives an effective power of 2,400 horses. There are 240 pairs of rollers in it on one floor; the rollers were made in Buffalo. The wheat is run through seven times, or rather through seven pairs of rollers, and the flour finished by ordinary stones. The whole concern works like a piece of clockwork, and turns out 7,000 barrels of flour in twenty-four hours. They have other mills, making their output altogether 10,500 barrels daily, or sufficient to feed two cities the size of New York. They have two immense elevators in Minneapolis for storing wheat, and have small ones at almost all the railway stations in the surrounding wheat districts, all in communication with the chief office by wire, so that supplies of wheat can be got along as required. They have a railway into the mills, and use two hundred trucks a day to take wheat into, and the productions of it out of, the mills. They have a fine system of precautions against fire: sprinklers which come into play at temperatures below fire heat, and tell-tales which give indication at a less high temperature. The water-power used in these mills as well as the mills belong to the Pillsburys, on whom I called, and found to be very nice people. Their agents in London are Messrs. W. Kline and Son, of Tower Street.

The one drawback is that for three months in the winter the sources of the river are frozen, and they are therefore obliged to have a stand-by in the shape of steam engines, which they use during that time. Everything that could be done to save labour was done; the casks were delivered at a spot where they rolled themselves into position and counted themselves. The sacks were put into a spout with a slope to it and then a slight rise, so that they sprung themselves into the conveyances used to remove them. No wonder our millers have a hard time of it with such competition, and I am afraid it looks like lasting. Of course this mill is only one of a number, but I suppose the largest. The best hotel in Minneapolis is large, new, and built of brick and stone. The buildings and shops are altogether excellent. We return to St. Paul in time for dinner, and leave to-night at 8.40 for Chicago.

We started as arranged and slept on the train. We got up at six and had a splendid breakfast in the dining-car at seven. The land about here is well fenced and beautifully cultivated. There are good-looking small towns every twenty or thirty miles. At 9.30 we arrived at Milwaukee, a fine city on Lake Michigan. There are docks and a good bit of lake shipping here. The town is more than half peopled by Germans, and has plenty of beer and other German characteristics about it. We just had time to look into the city, which seemed to be a well-built and thriving place. The country still resembles one of our own home counties in a prosperous time. The crops look very promising, fences, &c., well kept up, small woods between some of the fields, and just enough hill and water to give it a comfortable, pretty appearance. Of course this is a nice time of year, as the trees are well in leaf and the wild flowers plentiful.

Chicago was reached about noon, and the rest of the day was spent in looking round the best streets, which are mostly very wide. The buildings are many of them larger than we have in the City of London, and all are now built of stone and brick. The system of having lifts in all blocks of business premises enables them to be used though built very high; in fact, the best rooms are on the highest floors. Many of the business blocks have three and four lifts always at work, and the office rents seem to be about the same here as in the City of London. There is a little river running out of the lake through the town, and as it has a branch to it, it gives over twenty miles of water frontage, which is used for business purposes. But this river is an inconvenience to the town itself, as the bridges over it are constantly opening to let vessels through, and thus hindering the land traffic. The people, however, are getting over this difficulty by making tunnels under the river. Cost seems no object here. They have two already made, although this place has only been begun fifty years, and it has been destroyed once and very much damaged by fire on a second occasion, it is now a very well built city, having seven hundred thousand inhabitants, and some of the finest streets and drives I have ever seen. You would fancy you were in a large seaport town by the shipping and docks, instead of in an inland town on a lake. In the later part of the day we drove out about seven miles, to the park and racecourse. The park is new, but well laid out and kept, and of considerable extent. After dinner we went to Hooley's Theatre, built entirely of iron. The private boxes were more like cages of iron (ornamental, of course) than those we have in England. The American ladies do not seem to wish to be shut in, and in these boxes you can see them all round.

2nd.—This morning we called on Mr. Monier Williams and delivered the parcel we brought for him, and then went to the office of Mr. Armour, the great meat merchant. His office is in itself a curiosity and the picture of life and business, telegraphs and telephones going in all quarters, and an army of clerks all at work and open to view, Mr. Armour himself at a desk like the rest, and only to be distinguished by having a large bouquet of flowers near him. They gave us an order to go over the works, about six miles off, and we started at once.

The works are in the middle, or nearly so, of the vast stock-yards, covering, I should think three hundred acres or more. We were shown first into the pig-killing department, which is really a rather fearful place. Pigs are driven into a large pen, holding perhaps a hundred, where two men are engaged in placing a chain round one hind leg of each. They are then caught up by machinery and hoisted over a platform, where the executioner stands; he takes hold of one of their fore feet and cuts a gash in their throats, which at once makes them lose all the blood they have in them, and they slide along, still hung up, over a grating, and in less than a minute seem to be dead; at least, they have done squeaking and struggling. They then fall off into a long trough of boiling water, and are passed on by other dead pigs pressing on behind until they come to a machine which takes nearly all their hair off. What little remains is taken off by hand. They are then hoisted up and again passed on to another kind of executioner who severs the head all but a little piece. Further on, several more men turn to and disembowel them, and a number more sort and dress the refuse, and chop them in two down the spine; the halves then run by a little overhead railway into a large warehouse, where they hang from twenty-four to forty-eight hours, to cool and harden, after which they are cut up, and the parts prepared for sausages (which are made by machinery), or made into hams, or bacon, or whatever may be required.

In this way five thousand pigs a day are killed and cured, or, say, eight a minute. The bullocks are treated in a different way. There are several pens just large enough to hold a bullock alongside the dressing-house. They are driven in at one end, and a man, who stands on a platform on the top, shoots them through the brain with a small rifle-bullet, about the size of a pea; they take some little time to die, but do not appear to suffer much. Two thousand a day, or nearly two a minute, finish their existence in this way. We had seen enough of blood, and did not see the execution of the calves and sheep. The men are as strong as lions, and seem to enjoy their work. The whole place is unfit for any sentimental person to visit, but I suppose it is only concentrating the horrors of ordinary slaughterhouses. This firm sells meat, &c., to the value of 43,000,000 dollars, or nearly £9,000,000 per annum. There are several other firms of the same sort here, but not so large. They have twenty acres of refrigerating space to keep the meat ready for market, and everything else in proportion.

The number of cattle received in Chicago altogether is almost incredible.

We next drove to one of the large elevators, but not the largest. The wheat as it is sent into the towns is examined by a Government official, who pronounces it to be of either first, second, or third quality, and it is bought and sold in the market on these grades, so that a dealer never need see a sample. When the wheat is sent into store it arrives with a certificate giving the grade and year of growth. The owner of the elevator, which is in fact a storehouse, is not obliged to deliver the particular wheat any man sends him, but is obliged to deliver wheat of the same grade and year of growth. This arrangement simplifies the business very much. The elevators or storehouses are very large wooden structures, built up almost entirely of boards, the outside boards 8 inches by 2 inches, and the inside boards 4 inches by 2 inches; they are so piled and interlocked as to form a number of bins, which average, say, 15 feet square and 50 feet deep. These are so arranged that they can be filled by means of a Jacob's ladder lift from trucks below, and can be emptied by spouts into trucks or ships as required. The only thing the owner of the storehouse elevator has to do is to take care the grade and years' growth is kept separate, and that the weights in and out are correct.

The systems for lifting and weighing are very good. An elevator to hold 750,000 bushels, or say 100,000 quarters, costs nearly £100,000, at least so they say, but I should not have thought it. We drove round the docks and business part of the city, and afterwards walked to the lake, which, of course, looks like the ocean, as there are no shores to be seen on the opposite side. There were, however, ten good-sized vessels of different rigs in sight. I may remark the gasometers are all under cover in the towns we have lately passed through, as a protection from the frost.

The brick buildings are erected without scaffold, the bricklayers working from the inside, and laying the bricks overhand, as we build our chimneys.

We are altogether among the black waiters again. They are under better control here than farther south, but are rather a queer lot, and love a talk. I complimented one at St. Paul on the way he waited, when he made the remark that he certainly knew how to wait properly, but that his trouble was that so few of those he waited on knew how to eat properly.

This hotel (the Palmer House) deserves description. It is a very large building on one of the best streets; it has a large hall in the centre, where there are seldom less than one to two hundred people. Round it and leading out of it are three waiting-rooms, two telegraph offices, a railway ticket office, a café, beautifully fitted, hairdresser's shop, large enough for thirty or forty people to be attended to at once; large billiard saloon; chemist's shop, open all night; and a dozen other shops of different kinds. The hotel office has half a dozen attendants. It is paved with marble, and is lit by hundreds of electric lights. There is a double marble staircase, and there are two hydraulic lifts. Upstairs there is a dining-room fitted and decorated much like the large rooms at Versailles, with two smaller dining-rooms leading out of it. The corridors are very large and high, beautifully carpeted, with easy-chairs and seats at every convenient place. There are several drawing-rooms leading out of them, and above and around are eight hundred bed and sitting-rooms. Many of the bedrooms have bath-rooms with them, as ours has. There are between fifty and sixty coloured waiters, who are drilled like soldiers, and marched in and out of the room after inspection, and a small army of boot-blacks, porters, and servants. There are seldom less than a thousand people staying here; and there is a resident physician, with rooms on staircase landing. Such a place must require very good management to run it as this is worked.

In the evening we went to another very pretty theatre, decorated in the Eastern style, having little Eastern-looking balconies arranged so that the occupants of one could see the stage without any one else getting in the way, and with lights at back to throw out the tracery, which looked very pretty.

3*rd*.—We went round the docks and business premises, and afterwards took the train to Pullman, a town created entirely by the car-builder of that name. It is about sixteen miles out of Chicago, on the shore of a small lake. It is entirely given up to those engaged in the works. As you leave the station, which is an ornamental one, you go into the park, where the works stand, and past a piece of ornamental water having a fountain in it. The whole is kept as well as a private garden could be. The office-block is in the centre of the main front building. There is a notice up, "Public allowed to visit engine-room and tower" only. So I thought our journey had been in vain. However, I went to the manager, and, on presenting my card, and telling him we were from England, he gave us an order to visit all the shops, and what is more, and pleased us much better, the order passed us everywhere alone, so that we could poke about as we liked, and we had two or three hours real enjoyment. The works consist of three rows of buildings, one behind the other, with rows of rails, or what they call traversers, between each. These traversers are as wide as the sleeping-cars are long, and have a little engine attached to them, to enable the cars, in the different stages of progress, to be moved about from shop to shop, to receive the next stage of work. The front row of shops is a splendid pile of buildings. The machinery is driven by an engine of 1,500 horse-power, one very large shaft running the whole length. The engine-house is a large building, almost like a church, with ample room in it. It has several park seats, and an ornamental armchair, for the use of visitors. The wooden floor is kept as white as possible, and altogether it is quite a show place. The first buildings of the block are used for making paper wheels—that is, the centres of the wheels are made of paper. Discs of that material are piled together and compressed by very powerful hydraulic presses until they adhere, and become almost as hard as iron ; they are bolted on to the tyres and bosses very much as Mansell's wooden wheels are bolted on, having iron plates on either side, but so as to allow play for the elasticity of the paper. To me there seemed no very great advantage in it, but I suppose there must be or they would not be made. The car-making proper came on next : first the shops for cutting up and preparing all the different pieces of wood required for the framework. Then the shops for making all the fitting and cabinet work of the cars, and as this is very beautifully done (the carving and inlaid work being equal to any furniture I have ever seen) the machinery is proportionately fine, and several hundred men were employed at it. Then come the shops for putting all together, each shop taking a different branch of the work. The next row of buildings was given up to the preparation of the ironwork, which is very complicated and difficult, but the order of manufacture is preserved, as in the wood-work. Behind are the shops for the rougher work, such as making the bogies the carriages run on. There are also kilns for drying the timber, so that not the slightest shrinkage may be observed in the finished work. The works employ 6,000 men. The town is nicely laid out; in the best part there is a very fine hotel, built in the same style as the works—red and black bricks. The hotel has all necessary requirements, including a large barber's shop. There is a fine building containing lecture-hall, library, &c., the centre forming an arcade with shops which any town might be proud of. The houses for the managers are prettily designed, and have avenues of trees before them; behind are the houses for the workmen. Ten years ago the place was a swamp; the works were erected in three years, and have since been in full work. They are now largely increasing them. There is a staff of men whose whole duty it is to keep the place tidy and clean, and they have inspectors always going the rounds to see it is so.

We returned to Chicago to dinner, started at nine, had a good night in a sleeping car, and at six in the morning were at Detroit. Although the train ran to Montreal our sleeper was detached at Detroit, in order to give the occupants more sleep, as six is too early to turn out for business, so we were able to wash and shave in peace.

4th.—Detroit is situated on the American side of the Windsor river running between Lake Erie and Lake Huron, and thus connects the two great lakes. The river is about as wide as the Thames at Gravesend, but always at one level, and the current always setting towards Lake Erie, and thus supplying the water for the Niagara Falls. All the vessels trading between the different lakes have to pass here. The traffic reminds you of the Lower Thames, so numerous are the craft; but instead of ocean steamers there are very curious-looking ones, constructed for the lake traffic. The town is an important one, having 130,000 inhabitants, and very extensive manufactures. It is, moreover, very well laid out, paved and lighted, and seems to be as thriving as the other towns about here, which is saying a great deal. The train was put on to a large ferry boat and brought to the Canadian town of Windsor, on the other bank of the river. This is not a very large place, but fairly prosperous, I should think. We then passed through Chatham, and while I am writing this we are in London, so we ought to feel nearly at home. A man is in the carriage calling " London evening paper." Farther on we passed a very nice place, Port Hamilton, situated at the south-west point of Lake Ontario; it appears to be prosperous, and the country round is pretty. Between that and Niagara there are two canals, connecting Erie and Ontario, the old one only deep enough for a very light-draft craft, the new one taking vessels through of fourteen feet draught of water. It seems to me a very important matter to have a canal deep enough to allow any sized ocean steamers to pass through. It would allow trade to be carried on between the immense region round the shores of the lakes and the countries of the world without having to tranship the cargoes.

I expect the Canadians will have one before long; the States would have had one before this, I believe, had they been masters of the situation. The land in this part of Ontario is good and well cultivated, and the country altogether pretty and well-to-do, and has an undulating surface. We crossed the suspension bridge at Niagara in the train over the rapids, which are indeed wild. A man trying to swim them must be mad.

There are three bridges: a light suspension bridge near the Falls, a cantilever bridge, and the lower suspension bridge. The two last are the best structures.

The water was very high, and the cloud of spray from the Falls nearly hid them from our sight. Lake Erie was very much swollen, and many parts dry when we were last there, are now under water. Buffalo looked better, as the snow had vanished and the trees were in leaf. We spent a quiet Sunday with Charlie and Polly, and called on a few of the friends we had made. On Monday we took train for Boston, doing the chief part of the journey in the night. However, we were able to see some of the country in the morning. It is pretty, very rocky, with nice streams, and small trees, and sufficiently hilly to make it pleasing. There are also some fertile districts between the rocks, and some small lakes.

The city of Boston struck us as being very much like a good English town. The streets are not too regular, and there is a beautiful park, called the Common, in the middle of the town. The buildings are good, and there are certainly more pretty things to look at than in any of the newer cities—in fact, the place is riper and more to my taste. I expect the other American cities will get more like this place in time. Moreover it seemed to me the people were not in such a hurry, and have begun to realise there are other objects in life than simply making money. We had a good look round the business quarter and were much interested in the way the different fruits and vegetables came to market. They take more pains in packing them than we do; the strawberries, for instance, come in nicely made wooden trays, packed thirty-two in a large case, and so arranged that air can get to them and no one package can touch another. The thirty-two small trays, and the large packing-case to hold them, with divisions, &c., complete, are supplied by the maker at one dollar, or four shillings each. The beans, onions, and many other vegetables or fruits are supplied in little six-sided wooden cases. I should think they could be made cheaper than any packages used in England. The garb of the butchers also pleased me— trousers, vest, &c., were made in one piece of thin white material, and evidently clean on every morning; they were put on over their ordinary clothes. We came away to New York by the Fall River railway and boat. The railway took us about two hours; as we started from Boston about six, we arrived at the Fall River at eight. Whilst in the train we were handed, in exchange for our tickets, keys of the state-rooms we were to occupy on the boat. When we arrived at the wharf we found the boat *Bristol* there and a very nice dinner ready in her dining saloon. About two hundred and fifty of us sat down to first dinner, and afterwards went up to the main saloon, which was a splendid apartment, beautifully furnished and carpeted; it was very high, 20 feet or more, with a large gallery round it, and at one end a capital band, which played an excellent selection of music. There were between six and seven hundred sleeping berths in cabins round the different decks, an electric light in each, and a kind of double-story bedstead, with ample room; and on the lowest deck about twelve hundred second-class horsehair beds, without blankets or other clothing.

The vessel was brilliantly illuminated in all parts by electric lights, which were partly turned down about eleven, as a hint to go to bed, which we did. In the morning we got up between five and six o'clock and found ourselves well on the way to New York, having taken the East river passage between New York and Long Island. The remaining part of the journey was so pretty and interesting I could not go down to breakfast, although I ought to have had coffee in my berth at 5.30, and breakfast in proper saloon at seven.

However, we did very well by watching the boat find its way among the rocks and craft and through a district full of life and beauty until we got to our landing in New York, which we did at the appointed time, although great part of the night had been foggy.

9th.—We are back again in New York, which looks better now than it did when we first visited it. The day is hot and bright. We spent the morning in the park, which is well laid out and has some pretty pieces of water in it. We went over the museum and picture gallery, which is well worth seeing, although not yet up to those in most European cities. In the afternoon we wanted a blow, as it was hot, and so we took a steamer to Coney Island, a little place at the southern end of Long Island ten or twelve miles from New York, where there are several piers, music halls, &c. It is something in style between a French fair and Margate. The people of New York go there to spend a happy day, and there are some very strange amusements and buildings—among other things a house built in the shape of an elephant; and as it is very large—in fact, three or four times as high as any of the houses—it looks very peculiar.

There are also several enormous restaurants. Among other things we took note of at Boston were some launches driven by means of a small engine using naphtha. There was no boiler, but the naphtha was converted into gas and pressure as it was used, and after being used in the engine was condensed again and pumped back to the tank. The only heat used was a petroleum lamp. For a 25-feet launch the whole apparatus could not have weighed more than I could easily lift. I should say more will come out of this invention, as it could be applied to all sorts of power purposes. I saw one of the launches under way and she went remarkably well. I shall call at the factory, which is in New York.

10*th*.—On Friday we called at Captain Green's office. He had gone to the West, but had left us an order to see the new gas-engine, or rather an engine made for steam driven by ammonia gas. It seems water will hold a large quantity of ammonia at a low temperature, which it gives off at a higher temperature, and this at any pressure required, provided it is heated enough; and as it is more volatile than water, it gives the necessary pressure at a less temperature, and therefore saves fuel. After it is used in the engine it is exhausted into water of low enough temperature to hold it, and again pumped back into the boiler. That we saw working seemed to answer admirably; no smell of ammonia was noticeable. Of course all leakage had to be avoided, and brass-work to working parts removed and replaced by iron; but in this case there seemed to be no difficulty.

We then went to the Gas Engine and Power Company, 131st Street, Harlem River, where we saw the naphtha engines I spoke about as having been seen by us in Boston on launches. This invention is certainly a success. There is a tank of naphtha in the bow of the boat, which is led to the stern by a pipe. Part of it is burnt by a kind of lamp, which heats up a small quantity of the spirit, pumped out of the tank into a coil, and it is converted into vapour and pressure by the heat and passed through a little three-cylinder engine and exhausted into a pipe passing outside of the boat under the water-line, where it becomes cool again and returns to a liquid state, and is then pumped back into the tank and used over and over again. The engine takes about as much room as a man would sitting in the stern of the boat. They lent us a launch to take us up to the station, which was about a mile up the river.

The lamp was lit as we got on board and in less than two minutes we went off at a very good speed. I reversed the engine myself in a moment. She was so handy, you could run her at full speed, say eight or nine miles an hour, and by reversing the engine stop in her length. No arrangement has been made as to working this patent in England yet. The owner has promised to communicate with me previous to doing anything in it. I don't think it would be much trouble to get the works at Erith.

It is bound to be a success. They are working at the launches night and day, and have more orders than they can possibly execute. Moreover, I think the principle might be applied to other purposes without end. This and the ammonia engine indicate mediums for producing power from heat which may make some strange alterations during the next few years; and although both working in the same city, one was being worked out without the knowledge of the other.

11*th.*—This morning we started for home in the *Umbria*, a sister ship to the one we came out in. It is the pet voyage of the season; that is to say she carries nothing but first-class passengers, and has between five and six hundred on board. Her resources are taxed to the utmost. The string of carriages conveying passengers to the pier reached a long distance. Friends brought great baskets of flowers set up in all sorts of designs, in all enough to fill the big saloon. Some of the designs were full-rigged ships, with flowers for the sea and strings of flowers for ropes, and heavier than one man could carry. There were several cartloads of them altogether. The tables were covered with telegrams from friends wishing passengers a good voyage. The pier was crowded with friends, some having flags made on purpose to wave as we left. Then there were two steamers loaded with friends and having bands on each to accompany us to sea, the cheering and waving lasting an hour or more.

We were some time getting clear of Sandy Hook and the bar, but about 12 o'clock we put the pilot on board his boat and started the engines full speed. The vessel need not be described, as she is in all respects like the *Etruria*. The passengers are very much more numerous and consequently not quite so easy to know. As we knew how to manage, we secured seats at the centre table for the first set of meals, and also secured the turn we wanted for our morning bath. The voyage turned out not a very good one. Most of the passengers being ill and very difficult to please, food was served in any cabin and on deck all day, but most of the people only looked at it after they got it. I heard one steward ask a lady whether the beef-tea was to her liking, and when she told him it was just right, the man remarked, "Thank God, I have got it right once!" We had twenty-four hours fog off the Banks of Newfoundland. The water got very cold, so the engines were slowed, as ice was feared. The Captain was on the bridge all this time. He is an old weather-beaten sailor, and it was grand to hear him read the Church service beautifully on Sunday morning in the presence of many of the passengers and crew and several clergymen. Afterwards he asked one of them to address us, and the Rev. Dr. Hall, a leading Presbyterian clergyman of New York, gave us a short but good sermon. There is a bishop on board, but he did not take any part. During the voyage we made many acquaintances, and there was some heavy play in the smoking-room.

We had Sir Edward Thornton on board (formerly the British Ambassador to the

States), who I should think was a very nice man. But no one avoided conversation or put on airs, so that the voyage was a pleasant one, and with music and singing every evening we got on very well. On the last two days there was less motion and there were many fresh faces on deck, and those who up to now had looked the picture of misery began to dress up a bit and do their hair, and the men began to shave. By the time we reach Queenstown we shall be a fairly good-looking party, but one and all will be glad to get the voyage over.

18*th*.—We are to have a concert to-night. It is about the first time enough of the passengers have felt up to it. The concert came off, and very good it was; some of the comic songs were much beyond the average, and one man gave some excellent recitations. There was a collection afterwards for sailors' orphans, by which between £60 and £70 was raised. Queenstown was reached next day, the mails landed, and in a few hours more we were off Liverpool, but too late to land;

ARRIVING AT LIVERPOOL.

we therefore had to stay on board until Sunday morning.

The arrangements at the Customs were abominable; it took several hours to get through and then only by finding the different pieces of luggage ourselves and being our own porter. We found ours at last and an officer to look over and pass it. We carried it out to a cab, and as a crowning point a rough kind of porter followed us out and demanded so much a package, although he had not touched it. Of course I did not pay, but I daresay some of the strangers did, and I could not help feeling ashamed that such confusion and imposition should be possible, and that it should be the first introduction of many foreigners to our way of doing such things.

Before closing my diary I must give a few of the opinions I have formed of the people and the country of the United States.

The people are, I think, more lively, free, and enterprising than we are. There is no difficulty in approaching them. From the shoeblack to the most important men I have seen, they are well-informed and always ready and pleased to give information, even at some inconvenience to themselves; and this not from anything they expect in return, as, with the exception of the blacks, they never even thank you if you offer them anything. There is a certain air of equality about all of them, and they require as a first step that you should acknowledge this. The cabman talks to you not as a servant, but as an equal, and asks for information in exchange for what he can give you. The conductor of the train shows his authority at once in a civil sort of way, sits down in the opposite seat, and engages the passengers in conversation, whether they be ladies or gentlemen, and is always well-informed. He dines at the same table, has his bed made up, and is, although perfectly civil and obliging, entirely one of the party, having and expressing his opinion on all subjects; even the porters act very much in the same way. The better, or I should say, the better-to-do classes, are, as far as I have been able to know them, most courteous and obliging; they are very anxious to know your opinion of themselves and their country, and are a little hurt as a rule if it is not favourable in every instance. At the same time they almost one and all express some opinion more or less unfavourable to the institutions of England. In fact they are a little thin-skinned; they profess to have grown entirely out of the influence of their old mother England. It is natural enough her conservative ways should not suit them, and properly so too. The young blood starting in life for itself must strike out in a new direction, and I am rather inclined to think they have got the right one. Nevertheless they like the parents' approval, although they will not acknowledge it. The nation is, in my opinion, more vigorous in consequence of the admixture of German and other blood. There are a great number of Germans, and many French, Italians, and others, and a good deal of intermarrying; and this I am sure is good for the strength of the nation. The people in the country districts are very industrious; they go to bed early and are up by daylight. There may be drinking in the saloons, and I am told there is, but I have never seen anything like we have in England. They drink iced water, which is to be had in all public places and in every railway carriage. In the hotels nothing but water, tea, coffee, and milk is taken; not one in a thousand drinks wine or beer, and I did not see a man or woman the worse for liquor throughout the States. The women seem very self-dependent. They fill all sorts of situations, such as clerks and shorthand writers in offices, wait well at country hotels, and are entirely in earnest over their work. They, however, go their own way very much, constantly travelling alone, whether married or single.

The children are as a rule spoiled, and put their word in and give an opinion before they leave off pinafores, although they are good in travelling. They are mostly a little objectionable through being too forward.

The blacks are, as a race, improving, I should think. Some are well educated, well informed, and in good positions, but the great bulk of them in the South, I should fancy, are pretty much as they were in slave days, except that they are not slaves. The Indians are done for; they cannot live alongside the white man. The more they are studied the sooner they will become extinct, because, with a few exceptions, their rough life is a necessity to them, and being kept by the whites will only make them die out the faster. Those we saw at St. Augustine's were like caged animals. A few months in the fortress would destroy half of them. I think, on the whole, they are to be pitied, although they have very few good qualities to boast of.

The great size of the country can hardly be realised until you begin to travel over it. It includes all soils and all climates, from the mountains covered with perpetual snow to the semi-tropics, and consequently produces everything that can be wished for. Florida and South California produce oranges and all fruit that will grow in the temperature required for them. In the lower Mississippi Valley cotton and sugar-cane; and further north there is a wheat district almost without limit; while the cattle ranches can be established on the prairies running for more than a thousand miles each way. The timber districts are so extensive they have certainly made the impression on the people here that no amount of cutting, or waste, or destruction by fire will ever too far reduce them; but with this I cannot agree. There is a very large district in the north of New Mexico, which I should think never can be profitably cultivated; but even here minerals are found.

Then there is a supply of coal easily obtained all over the States, and some of it very good, to say nothing of that wonderful production, natural gas, which in some districts has superseded coal. They seem to have found every mineral but tin. Gold and silver are found in larger quantities than in any other country. Brick earth and slate do not appear to be plentiful, although I have seen some very good of both. The only thing I have not seen is tin and chalk. Grapes grow splendidly in California, and some of the wine is very good. I heard of one vineyard of over two thousand acres, and the wine made from it is fast gaining a name.

In the Southern States there are very large districts to be had at a nominal price, but my idea would be to buy land in Upper California, Oregon, or Washington. From San Francisco to the upper part of Washington territory there is a fertile country, with a good climate, to be had for next to nothing, and it is certain to grow in value in a few years; and the rivers there are not to be surpassed in the world.

The railways, all but those round the principal eastern cities, are single lines, and are not fenced in, and cross one another on a level. There is scarcely any system of signals, but the telegraph is depended upon alone. They run the trains, on an average, not much over twenty miles an hour, but sometimes thirty-five or forty. The bridges are much lighter than ours, and in the western districts are mostly made of timber. The railway carriages I like for travelling long distances. There is more freedom of action; you can walk from one end of the train to the other, shift your seat, or ride on the platform. They will let you jump up and down when the train is going, it being your own look-out if you are hurt. The sleeping-carriages enable you to do long journeys without being fatigued. You can have your bed made up when you like.

They are like the berths on a ship—one over the other. The upper one folds up in the daytime and contains the clothes, &c., and when closed forms part of the roof, and could not be noticed by a stranger. It is a little difficult to dress and undress, as you have to do most of it in your berth, where there is only just room to sit up, and it requires a bit of an education. There is a nice retiring-room and washing-room at one end of the carriage for ladies, and another at the other end for gentlemen. It is, however, a little awkward having the ladies and gentlemen so mixed in sleeping; and as one pair of curtains protects both the upper and lower berth, it is almost impossible to get out of the top berth without disturbing the lady in the lower one. Moreover, you have to be very careful not to drop any part of your clothes over the side.

They have racks for small things, and hooks for coats, &c., but you cannot very well put them entirely out of your way. I think it would be better to divide the carriages into two at night, giving one part up to the ladies and the other to the gentlemen. They have on some lines just put on some new carriages having also baths and barbers' shops in them. It is the fashion among wealthy people to have private carriages put on the rails, and live in them. One gentleman on the *Umbria* told me he had, with three friends, been round the States in one which had parlour, sleeping-berths, kitchen, and servants' apartments in it. They got it to

San Francisco and wanted to come home by the Canadian Pacific, as we did, but as there is no railway up the west coast they went on by boat and sent the carriage back and round the other way to meet them at Vancouver, which it did after a journey of between four and five thousand miles. This was an English gentleman. His way of travelling had not enabled him to mix much with the people, and he had consequently not formed such a favourable impression of them generally as I have done. The ordinary roads all through the States, with one or two exceptions, are as bad as they can be, both in town and country. This quite spoils the appearance of some districts and renders the comparison between them and similar districts in England most unfavourable to the States, but we must remember that the railways are their high roads. Electricity is used in every way much more than in Europe. Telephones are used everywhere, and it surprised me very much to hear a woman in a little roadside house in the

Sierra Nevada Mountains, many miles off the railway-station, blowing some one up for not informing her of the number of passengers likely to arrive by the stage, as she had not prepared enough dinner for them. The telephone-wire, we found out afterwards had been hung on the fir-trees through the forest. There are a very large number of Roman Catholics in the States. Priests have the usual power over the people, and in some cases use it badly.

The churches are numerous and well supported, but, as far as I could find, the preachers are obliged to preach and act in such a way as to make themselves popular with the members of the congregation, and are in consequence not so independent as might be desirable. The pew sittings are sold by auction from time to time in most of the churches, and the more popular the preacher the more they fetch. Almost every man, woman, and child can read and write, and almost every one can express him or herself readily and to the purpose.

As since visiting Pittsburg I have obtained some more information about the natural gas which abounds in that district, I make a note of it here. The whole subsoil of Western Pennsylvania is more or less permeated with natural gas. It is stored up in the sandstone, and is generally found in the neighbourhood of petroleum or salt water. The depth of the wells varies from one thousand to four thousand feet. It was first used in working iron in 1874.

Its existence has been proved in twelve other States, but as yet it is not found there in sufficient quantities to be of much use.

Some seem to think it has been formed for ages and stored in the sandstone, where it is sealed up by rock so that it cannot get out until it is tapped. Others think it must be formed by the action of salt water (which is known to exist, and which may have found its way in from the ocean) on the carbon, which lies at various depths in the earth. All this seems but conjecture.

The supply, all agree, must sooner or later

be exhausted. In many cases wells have already failed, and in almost all cases the supply becomes less and less as time goes on. As a rule, the shallowest wells have the shortest existence.

The pressure at which the gas comes to the surface is in some instances enormous; in a few cases nearly 1,000 lbs. to the square inch, and in many over 500 lbs. This, of course, renders it difficult to control, and makes it almost impossible to prevent waste.

They have some plans for preventing it blowing off, but it is very difficult to get anything that will stand the pressure.

The companies have a regular scale of charges for the gas—so much for each ton of iron puddled, so much for use for a certain-sized boiler per month, and so on. An iron-master told me the charges worked out, as nearly as he could get at it, from 5 cents to 6 cents, or $2\frac{1}{2}$ to 3d., per 1,000 cubic feet at ordinary gas pressure.

One company, the Philadelphia, supplied last year over one thousand boilers, one thousand four hundred furnaces, many hundreds of other manufacturing heats, besides heating four thousand five hundred houses. The daily consumption was 182,000,000 cubic feet, which took the place of 10,000 tons of coal. This company alone has between three and four hundred miles of pipe laid, varying from 24 inches down to 6 inches in diameter. The total length of pipe laid in Western Pennsylvania is estimated at one thousand miles.

The gas is used at all pressures, varying from 50 lbs. to 2 ounces per square inch, but the most usual pressure is 1 lb. to the square inch. The exact quantity of air to mix with the gas, so as to get the best results, is ascertained by experience, and varies a little with different work. There are also many kinds of furnaces, some giving better results than others. In glass-manufacture, particularly, the use of this gas gives results not to be got by any other known method.

It struck me forcibly as being the most wonderful and useful natural production I had ever seen. It is cleaner, cheaper, and more easily used than coal; it conveys itself along the pipes to the places where it is wanted, can be lit in a moment, will produce any required heat, and its use can be discontinued by turning a tap. The manufacturers are so pleased with it that one and all of those who spoke to me about it told me they should certainly put up gas-producers if the natural gas failed, as after once using the gas they could not go back to coal with any comfort.

Last year there were sixty-five companies for the supply of natural gas in Pennsylvania, with a capital of over 50,000,000 dollars, or £10,000,000 sterling.

The cost of drilling a gas-well varies from 3,000 to 6,000 dollars, according to the depth. A derrick is first erected, and a wrought-iron pipe driven through the soft earth until it reaches the rock. The drills weigh, with the "jars," 3,000 to 4,000 lbs. These rise and fall four to five feet, turning constantly, so as to bring the bit in contact with the entire circumference of the hole. An 8-inch hole is bored to a depth of say five hundred feet, and a $5\frac{3}{8}$ inch casing put down to shut off the water. The hole is continued 6 inches in diameter until gas is struck, when a 4-inch pipe is put down. From forty to sixty days are required for drilling a well.

The Government. Well, unless I am careful I shall be saying something I do not understand; but, as far as I can understand it, each State has in theory entire control over nearly all its internal affairs—railways, and all public works, liquor laws, divorce, and the life and death of its people, and in fact can do almost anything an independent nation can do, except putting on protective duties as against other States or foreign countries; and had even the power of withdrawing from the Union. The consequence is that in travelling through the country as we have been doing it may be perfectly legal to do something at one minute which at the next may be punishable by imprisonment. This is no exaggeration, as in some States you can buy and sell spirits or shoot game, and then just over the border both be treated as crimes. Then each State has control of the army raised in it until it is wanted to fight for the general good of the Union, when it is under the control of the Central Government. Every year, however, seems to modify the relations between the individual States and the Central Government, and this, I think, must be so, as intercourse becomes greater. Even now there is a great talk as to the action of an Inter-State Commerce Bill, which over-rides the separate States and controls all the railways; and the question as to the power of any State to retire from the Union was settled in the negative by the slave war. What must happen, I think, is that the law-making in some very important matters will be centralised, and that the institutions must so far be made more to resemble ours; and as I suppose our course of legislation will be in the other direction, and that we shall before long have county boards and local self-government in many ways; perhaps twenty years will find the institutions of the two Governments more alike than most people now think they are likely to be. I fancy politicians would do well to make a study of the progress of the States in law-making, as many questions which before long will be of prominent importance—such as the relation of labour to capital—may first be fought out over there.

I am myself so far interested in the country and government that my trip and the information I have gained will, I am confident, have a distinct influence on my thoughts and judgment in the future, and I am therefore very pleased that I made up my mind to give up three months to a visit to the most interesting of the modern countries of the world—the United States.

www.ingramcontent.com/pod-product-compliance
Lightning Source LLC
Chambersburg PA
CBHW020822230426
43666CB00007B/1066